PUT IT
ON THE HOUSE
WHY HOME PRICES WILL SOAR

13781 NE 2nd Place
Bellevue, WA 98005
425-830-0198

Second Edition April 2012

Cover art by Gabriela Bloom
Book design by Grace Maher

PUT IT
ON THE HOUSE
WHY HOME PRICES WILL SOAR

By Edward S. Harris

PUBLISHED BY
QUAIL LANE BOOKS

To Gabriela, Sam and Izzy, who more than anyone have taught me the true meaning of wealth.

And in memory of Max, our family's beloved puppy. Ten years wasn't nearly enough, but we cherished every moment we had together.

Table of Contents

Who is rich? He who rejoices in his portion.
Rabbi Ben Zoma, *Pirkei Avot*, Chapter Four

Introduction

The time to buy is when there's blood in the streets.
Baron Rothschild

My family and I live in Bellevue, Washington. Our community, once merely a sleepy suburb of Seattle, is now a major business center in its own right, with a population of over 100,000 and a booming local economy. Downtown Bellevue sports new office towers, upscale restaurants, luxury stores (including the only Neiman-Marcus in the state of Washington) and gleaming new condos and apartments. Microsoft occupies over one million square feet of brand new commercial office space in Bellevue in addition to its sprawling suburban campus one town over in Redmond.

Our house sits on property that was developed about sixty years ago, when Bellevue truly was a distant suburb, at a time when the streets were rolled up after eight pm. In those pre-Starbucks, pre-Microsoft, pre-Amazon days Seattle barely registered on the national consciousness and local land was cheap.

The Harris family abode was built by our next-door-neighbor.[1] He's a contractor, and in the late 1990's he moved with his family into a modest house sitting on a large piece of property just as the local real estate market began to heat up. He subdivided the land, and built two new McMansions side-by-side. We moved into our (over-sized) home in August 2000, at a time when the national economy was going strong and Seattle was absolutely sizzling, thanks largely to its booming technology sector.

Fast forward about a year, to 9/11 and its aftermath. In a one-two punch, the Internet bubble popped like a soap bubble on a summer day, leading to a precipitous, lurching crash of the Nasdaq and sending hundreds of dotcoms to oblivion. All of a sudden, Seattle, rain-soaked land of technology billionaires, was struggling. I was reminded of the speed of the boom/bust cycle of Wall Street, where

---

1 The nice neighbor, not the other one.

I started my career[2] fresh out of business school.

It was during this mini-economic apocalypse that I noticed two new homes being built a few blocks away. This project struck me as a bit odd, for a couple of reasons. My family and I live near a major local arterial, about two hundred yards down a private lane. This small bit of distance doesn't sound like much, but it creates a wonderful buffer from traffic. When you step out our front door you see a handful of other homes with driveways and front yards, a bucolic vision of American suburbia.[3] But these two new homes under construction were being built right on a main road, situated just a few feet away from constant, heavy traffic. Even worse, they were next to an electrical substation, which was only partially obscured by some newly planted trees. And, they were sitting practically at the corner of a busy intersection of criss-crossing four-lane roads, almost directly opposite a Walgreens and across from a gas station.

2 Two jokes from my investment banking days following a massive round of industry layoffs in the late '80's: What do you call an investment banker? "Waiter." And, what does an investment banker usually say? "Do you want fries with that?"

3 Except for our front lawn, which we allow to go brown in the oxymoronic dry Seattle summers.

Just as wearing shorts and a tee shirt isn't a lot of clothing but is still quite different than walking around naked,[4] being a good three-wood away from a main thorough-fare on a private lane, makes a world of difference as compared to living right on a busy street. I couldn't imagine why anyone would shoehorn these two houses into a site that seemed totally inappropriate for upscale homes, and I had even more difficulty imagining any buyers foolish enough to purchase them. Still, in 2003 when construction for this new project was finished and the builder starting holding open houses, I decided to go over and take a look for myself. To my surprise, I discovered that on a square footage basis, these new McMansions were priced about 20% higher than ours. I remember shaking my head and thinking to myself "are they on drugs?" I figured that to buy a $1.3 million house, you need at least $300,000 in down payment and closing costs, and then would be taking on a $1 million mortgage. Who, I wondered, with that kind of liquidity and income would take the plunge to buy such

4 New Jersey outlaws dancing in clubs in which body parts that would "normally be covered by a bikini" are exposed.

obviously (to me, at least) over-priced houses in an otherwise weak economy?

These two houses did eventually sell. They sit there today, hard by the substation and the Walgreens. The newly planted trees have grown enough to create some visual privacy, and presumably the owners either have gotten used to the road noise or keep the windows closed.

These two particular houses that caught my attention weren't just a local phenomenon. It turns out America was just beginning to enter a national mania over the housing market that almost perfectly mirrored the mania over dotcom stocks, and ended of course just as disastrously.[5] Despite considering myself financially sophisticated, I had at the time never heard of subprime mortgages, a term that would soon be front page news. I assumed that any buyer at this price would have to have lots of available cash for a down payment and a high level of steady income to make the mortgage payments. Oh, how naïve I was!

5 When it comes to economic cycles, history *does* repeat itself, a fact we will discuss later in the book.

About a year later, I was chatting with the neighbor who built our house.[6] He casually mentioned that he had taken out a new home equity line of credit, which seemed prudent to him, because, he said, "Homes go up in value by about 10% every year."

I thought about that comment afterwards. If home prices went up by 10% every year, as if this were a law of nature, they would become increasingly more valuable relative to other assets, and monthly mortgage payments would perpetually become more expensive relative to incomes. There is an old saying on Wall Street: "Trees don't grow to the sky." In short, in the world of business and finance, nothing goes up forever. In this case, the housing boom ran for a few more years, until the shaky mountain of risky mortgage debt it was built upon ran dry, and then the inevitable collapse occurred. That collapse has been one of the major economic stories for the last several years. Houses got inflated to preposterous values, a massive wave of overbuilding ensued, buyers took

6 As mentioned before, this is the good next-door-neighbor, not the other one, of whom the less said, the better.

out loans they had no ability to repay as unscrupulous mortgage brokers promoted the hype, and now our nation is absolutely awash in foreclosures, bankruptcies, and a banking system that is barely surviving on life support from the Federal Reserve. Chances are that you, dear reader, do not go three days without seeing a headline about foreclosures, underwater mortgages or the depressed real estate market.

Housing is in crisis, the economy is in terrible shape, and because a robust economy requires a healthy level of construction activity, we're all screwed.[7] This has become a business news mantra.

All of this is taken today as common knowledge. But, one of the "facts" about the housing crisis surprisingly is not true. Yes, home prices reached levels that were unsustainable, and brokers, lenders, builders and everyone else who stood to profit from increased sales promoted the boom as much they could for as long as possible. But one storyline about the housing bubble is actually incorrect: that there was a wave of overbuilding.

7 I promise to keep offensive language to a minimum.

Not only was there no overbuilding, if anything levels of construction have been so weak that the biggest problem we'll soon face is a housing *shortage*, not a surplus.

That we are in the early stages of this shortage is, fundamentally, the premise of this book. The reason is not because markets failed, but because they worked. As housing prices collapsed, construction activity, which relies on lending and investment capital, collapsed even faster, and stayed at depressed levels for years. As a result, we are looking at a genuine under-supply of housing that will lead to increased construction and help drive a robust recovery.

But I'm getting ahead of myself. I am going to walk you through a detailed economic analysis that I hope you will find compelling. Economics can at times seem like an overly dry subject, making best sellers on the topic quite rare.[8] Economists, like prognosticators of all types, are quite skilled at telling you what happened in the past, yet usually are not very good

8 Man, am I jealous of those two guys who wrote *Freakonomics*. I hope to tap into the same vein.

at predicting the future.[9] But, basic economic analysis can be a powerful predictive tool. In the case of housing the message is quite simple: the worst is over, and it's safe to go back in the water.

Over the chapters ahead, I hope to convince you that while most of what you know about the housing crisis is true, what has been reported in the press is accurate but incomplete. The real story is simple and powerful. This argument requires a careful analysis of certain statistics, but I have kept the charts and tables to a minimum. This book is not intended to be an academic discussion of market theory, but a basic dose of common sense. You might regard it as the explanation of why it is in the real world that trees *don't* grow to the sky. But, just as the basic fundamental workings of economics explain why goods and

9 Before Super Bowl XXXXII, football analysts were able to offer the following startling insight: the New England Patriots were only the second team in modern history to go undefeated during the regular season, and has already beaten their opponent, the NY Giants, a few weeks earlier. The Giants, on the other hand, were a wild card team who had lost six games. All the experts predicted that the Patriots would win handily, which was reflected in the betting line which had them as two-touchdown favorites. The Giants won. I experienced sports fan-orgasm. So much for the experts. And then for good measure they went and did it again in Super Bowl XXXXVI, leading to another sports fan orgasm.

services cannot become infinitely more expensive in real terms – i.e., relative to inflation or incomes – the reverse is true as well. Prices for basic commodities such as housing also cannot go *down* forever. In the case of housing, we have reached, or nearly reached, that floor and have nowhere to go but up.

I hope that my argument will prevail on merit. But at the risk of being slightly immodest[10], let me describe my professional background, in hopes that you may consider me a credible source. I have a B.A. from Rutgers in Economics with a minor in Hebraic Studies.[11] I worked as a pension actuary for one year – thank God it was only a year! – and then earned an MBA from Columbia University. I then spent five years in investment banking, working on mergers and acquisitions and financings for major companies such as British Airways and General Motors. In 1990, my family and I relocated to Seattle, and after two years in aviation finance, I have worked for the past twenty years in venture capital and technol-

---

10 As Golda Meir used to say, "Don't worry about being modest. You're not that great."

11 Apropos of absolutely nothing, I'd like to share with you that my favorite wine is Manischewitz.

ogy. I was part of the management team of a wireless communication company that was acquired by AT&T, an Internet company that was acquired by Disney, and was the co-founder of an online high school that was acquired by the parent of The University of Phoenix, The Apollo Group. Along the way, I spent a few years helping manage the personal investment portfolio of Paul Allen, co-founder of Microsoft. I also have been an active investor, and for a time published equity research with a boutique advisory firm I ran, Razor Capital, where my most memorable stock pick was Apple at under $30 per share.[12]

When it comes to common sense, I doubt if there is anyone who possesses more of it than my wonderful wife, Anne. I owe her a tremendous debt of gratitude for many things, including making sure our house is truly a home. And not just any home, but one of warmth and love, and where three two-legged children and one four-legged one (may his memory be a blessing) were molded into a family. And those children have been a

---

12 I've had my share of duds, too.

valuable lesson in economics themselves, including a primer in why a paycheck never seems to stretch far enough. Which leads me to another fundamental economic truth: buy this book!

Chapter 1: A Word of Advice

The minority is sometimes right;
the majority always wrong.

George Bernard Shaw

The collapse in housing prices has reached a point where it is just as extreme as the bubble that preceded it. Only a few years ago, all of the experts predicted home prices would continue to rise and that housing was a great investment. Unfortunately, that advice was deeply flawed, on a par with noted economist Irving Fisher's statement on Oct. 17, 1929, on the eve of the "Black Tuesday" crash some twelve days later, that stocks had reached a "permanently high plateau."

Over the last few years advice about the housing market has been like the Amityville Horror: "For God's sake, get out!" Don't buy a house. Rent, move back in with your parents, downsize, anything besides taking on ownership of a home. Mortgages are poison. Real estate is doomed. Save your immortal soul before it's too late.[13]

But this current belief, to permanently banish the thought that a house could possibly increase in value, and to avoid buying a home until prices come down even further, is as badly flawed as the longstanding and irrational optimism that preceded it.

My thesis is as follows: as of the publication of this book in early 2012, the US housing market is at or very near the bottom of a brutal decline that is unprecedented in modern times. Homes have declined in value on a national basis by about one-third, wiping out seven trillion (trillion!) in home equity. In the most depressed markets prices are down as much as 60-70%. About 30% of homeowners are underwater, meaning they owe more on their mortgages than the value of their house. Roughly ten million borrowers have been foreclosed on by their lenders over the last three years, and there may be millions more to come, as the sheer volume of delinquent mortgages has overwhelmed the system.

13 The careful reader will recall that in the Introduction I shared that I minored in Hebraic Studies, and have always had a keen fascination with religion. Which reminds me of a joke: Why do Methodists frown on pre-marital sex? Because it can lead to dancing.

Oh, and in case anyone forgot, the economy has been staggering over the weight of a massive recession that at its worst took the national unemployment rate to 10.1%, a level that would have been considered unimaginable just a few years ago.

Yet, despite all of this doom and gloom, I maintain that now is absolutely a great time to buy a home, and, if you have an investment portfolio, an equally good time to buy housing-related stocks. This may seem counter-intuitive, but I believe that a careful examination of the data will convince you. Perhaps you wonder if I must be smoking something funny. But there's nothing more mood altering in me than a steady flow of caffeine coursing through my system, a statement which would not have been true some thirty-five years ago.[14]

Please bear in mind that I am making a long term prediction. The collapse in housing values has been extraordinarily severe, and it's not inconceivable that prices could still come down a little bit more for a little while longer. I strongly believe that we are close

---

14 I inhaled.

to a bottom, but there may be a moderate amount of decline still ahead of us. With values down one-third nationally and over 60% in the most depressed markets, another decline of similar magnitude[15] is unlikely, unless we are reduced to living in caves and eating road kill. But there is no reason that another drop of 3-5% couldn't occur. Predicting an exact bottom is impossible, but also unnecessary. The key is that if you have a long term perspective, which almost by definition you need to have to commit to buying a house (or making an investment in the stock market), then being correct about the long term trend is the key to success. Houses today, as measured by affordability, comparison to renting, historical trends, or any other reasonable metric, are cheap. That doesn't mean they couldn't get a little cheaper before they start their inevitable long term rise.

Just like the Viagra ads say that one should consult their doctor to determine if getting laid, er, that is, if sexual activity, is good for them, one should similarly

15 Many foreclosed homes in Detroit are on the market for less than $10,000.

also pause to consider whether your own circumstances support owning a home or investing in real estate. If you do, then now is a great time to buy. And, if you have a 401(k) or investment portfolio and are a long term investor, then I believe buying stocks that will participate in a real estate recovery could produce solid profits in the years ahead. Now, I hope to persuade you that I am correct.

Chapter 2: Housing and Economics

If ignorance paid dividends, most Americans could make a fortune out of what they don't know about economics.
Luther H. Hodges

It's not for nothing that economics was dubbed by Thomas Carlyle "the Dismal Science." I was an economics major as an undergraduate – don't hold it against me – and can tell you that in fact it is an interesting discipline[16], providing fascinating insights into human behavior. Much like only evolutionary processes can explain the natural history of the earth and the diversity of life on our planet, so too only economic theory can explain the working of markets and the influence of financial factors on decision making.

Let's examine the nature of products that are built for sale. Economists differentiate between two types, based on their expected life: durable and non-

---

16 I was also on the Math team in high school, so you might take what I regard as interesting with a grain of salt.

durable goods. Durable goods such as cars, appliances, furniture and houses are expected to have a useful life of three years or longer. Non-durable goods, or consumables, have an expected life of three years or less.

The difference between these categories of goods is also reflected in the supply chain behind them. It does not take a lot of capital investment or logistical planning to ramp up production of non-durable goods. If demand increases for, say, cargo shorts, in response to a sudden new fashion trend, it's relatively easy for producers to ramp up output. For less than $25,000 of capital, you or I could rent space, buy some commercial grade sewing equipment, procure materials, and be in the cargo shorts business practically overnight.

It's quite a bit different for durable goods. Building airplanes or cars, for example, requires a massive amount of capital investment. A modern automotive factory costs in excess of $1 billion and takes years of planning to complete. Even for big companies, a billion dollars is a lot of money.[17]

17 As the late US Senator Everett Dirkson said, "A billion here, a billion there, and pretty soon it starts to add up to real money."

Consider the example of the airline industry. Probably no industrial commodity requires larger factories or more funding to generate output. A single widebody aircraft such as a Boeing 787 or Airbus A340 can cost in excess of $200 million. I spent a few years early in my career in aircraft finance (yes, it's as boring as it sounds). The airlines had gone through a deep slump in the 1970's due to high fuel prices and global recession. Aircraft makers sharply cut back production. Boeing, which at the time dominated the Seattle economy to an even greater extent than the automotive industry once ruled Detroit, laid off over 100,000 workers and a billboard near their main plant was put up which read "Will the last person who leaves Seattle please turn out the lights?" In the 1980's, when the global economy began to pick up, airlines scrambled to add more planes to their fleets. However, in the first few years of the recovery, production could not keep up with demand, and for a time in the late 1980's, delivery slots, that is the right to step into another airline's purchase contract and take possession of an aircraft when it came off the production line, were selling for over $5 million. It was the airline equivalent of ticket scalping.[18]

There probably is no type of product that is more "durable" than a house. Probably maintained, it can last for a century or longer. But housing is expensive and it takes a long time to create new supply. Unlike producers of non-durable goods, it is impossible for a builder to respond to increased demand by quickly ramping up production. The entire cycle, from the starting point of getting a building permit to driving in the last nail, can take years. Just preparing raw land for construction by laying roads, sewers and other required infrastructure can take more than a year. As a result, the ability of the housing market to respond to an increase in demand with more inventory for sale requires a considerable length of time. In a downturn, construction can be stopped immediately, especially if the builder goes

18 If there ever was a law that made absolutely no sense, it is the ban on selling tickets for more than their original price. Of all of the thousands upon thousands of goods and services sold in a modern economy, why tickets? If you go to a concert, you can resell the tee shirt you buy in the arena on eBay and be applauded for your financial acumen, but reselling the ticket is illegal. This is not an argument about legalizing prostitution or the sale of organs for transplant, for goodness sake. To paraphrase Allen Iverson, "It's just tickets."

bankrupt and the project runs out of money. But in an upturn, if more people want to buy houses, it's going to take years to meet that demand, and in the interim prices will go up.[19]

Housing is a fundamental human need, and has no substitute. As a species, we made a fateful evolutionary choice in prehistory to stand upright on the African savannah and become a two-legged hominid. Our brains grew, we developed language, we learned to hunt in groups, we lost our fur, our jaws became less powerful, and we even developed stomachs that help digest our food outside of our bodies – the process of cooking. We became weaker as individuals but more powerful as a species. A small band of scrawny humans can bring down a mastodon, a true triumph of brains vs. brawn.

Everything about our evolutionary history, including the fact that most of us no longer live in small tribes as hunter-gatherers on the African savannah, means that a human is unable to give up shelter from

19 Because, just to remind you, price is what balances supply and demand. Expect a question on this on the mid-term.

the elements. Life, human life, is simply inconceivable without a home, whether it's a cave, a tent or a suburban split level with a backyard and a swimming pool. Housing is as basic a human need as food and demand for new housing as population grows (much more on this later) is a permanent feature of the human condition.

Of course, as stated above, prices are determined by a combination of *supply* and demand. All this talk about the intrinsic human demand is fine, but, dear reader, what about the over-supply of houses built during the boom, you are thinking. Well, it's a fiction. In the chapters ahead I will show you that contrary to conventional thinking, we actually are facing a shortage of housing in the US, not a surplus.

Chapter 3: The Past: The Overbuilding Myth

It is a capital mistake to theorize before one has data. Insensibly one begins to twist facts to suit theories, instead of theories to suit facts.

Sherlock Holmes

When one reads articles or hears news reports about the housing crisis, the following terms come up repeatedly: subprime mortgages, foreclosures and over-building. The first two are abundantly true and supported by hard data, anecdotal evidence and economic logic.

Realtors get paid a commission when a house sells, mortgage brokers get paid when they underwrite a loan, lenders book instant profits when they bundle loans into securities, and Wall Street makes money when they sell these mortgage-backed securities to inves-tors. The entire system is set up so that every party is financially incentivized to sell as many houses and originate as many mortgages as possible. The larger the volume of transactions and the higher the prices, the bigger the profits. That people respond to financial incentives is self-evident: have you ever heard of a sales person who doesn't work on commission, or a big discount on a popular item that doesn't stimulate demand?[20]

During the bubble, home buyers were offered teaser loans with super-low payments ("option ARMs", aka "exploding" ARMs) and told not to worry about the fact that in a year or two a higher rate would kick in, because by then the value of their house would have gone up and they could simply refinance, which just translates to another round of profits for all the intermediaries: realtors, mortgage brokers, lenders and Wall Street. The stories that one reads in the news are all depressingly similar: when the merry-go-round came to a halt, borrowers discovered they couldn't afford their new, higher monthly mortgage payment, the value of their house had gone down, so they couldn't refinance, investors

20 Until recently I had never heard of the designer Missoni, largely because I am excruciatingly boring, and thereby much of modern life passes me by. When this famous designer whose items can go for over $10,000, made a line of low-priced goods exclusively for Target available as a special offer on September 13, 2011, the overwhelming volume of demand caused Target's website to crash and stores to sell out in minutes.

learned their mortgage-backed securities were junk debt despite triple-A ratings, and the global banking system nearly collapsed from the massive size and suddenness of the losses.

All of that is true, and foreclosures and the de-pressed state of the housing market still makes the news. But where is the evidence of overbuilding? Yes, undoubtedly in certain local markets such as Florida and parts of California there was too much construction, especially of particular types of properties, such as new sub-divisions on the periphery of a region and miles from anywhere, or high-rise luxury condos that suddenly had no buyers. But, was there systemic overbuilding such that an excess supply of houses that will create an overhang for years to come? The answer is a resounding "no."

Consistent and reliable data on housing goes back to 1959, over fifty years, nearly the entirety of the post-war period. If you think of a modern economy, with cars, factories, jet travel, a growing population, new industries and technologies, expanding international trade, a growing proportion of Americans going to college, and the ending of discrimination against blacks and women, then this period completely encapsulates the modern era. The 1960's may have been a while ago, but they weren't the 1860's. I grew up during this time[21], in an air-conditioned suburban home, spent a lot of time in the back seat of a car; we bought our groceries at a supermarket, watched a lot of TV, and I took the SAT to get into college. Today, my kids are growing up in a suburban home, spend a lot of time in the back seat of car; we buy our groceries at the supermarket, watch a lot of TV, and my kids need to take the SAT to get into college, the same colleges that were around back then.

So we are starting with like data, meaning comparisons from today to a few decades ago are statistically valid. Let's begin by looking at the number of new housing starts over the period from starting 1959 and ending in 2007, which is when the first signs

21 I was eleven years old when Playboy made the switch from topless photographs to full frontal nudity. It was a great time to be a developing adolescent male in America.

of the housing bubble began to emerge. I've presented the information in decades, except for the period of 2000-2007, supposedly the height of the real estate bubble, which I divided into two four-year periods, 2000-2003 and 2004-2007.

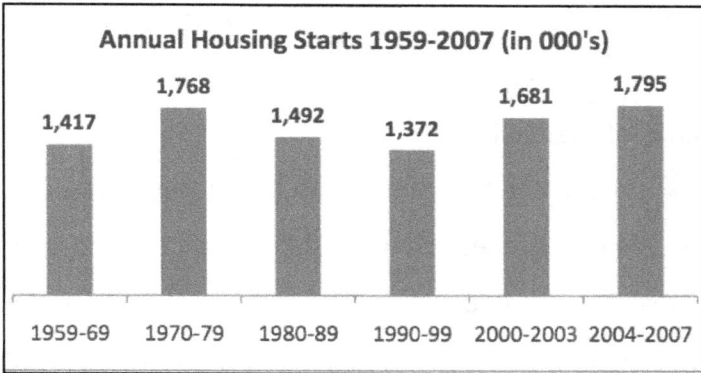

Annual Housing Starts 1959-2007 (in 000's)

1959-69	1970-79	1980-89	1990-99	2000-2003	2004-2007
1,417	1,768	1,492	1,372	1,681	1,795

Figure 1: Source: US Census Bureau

As you can see from Figure 1, the level of activity over this period has been remarkably stable. The US economy averaged about 1.4 – 1.8 million new housing units per year, in a consistent pattern, over a nearly fifty-year period of time. I have not yet introduced any demographic data, such as population or birth rates.

As I do so, the case that no overbuilding took place will become even more compelling. But for now, note that while you can see a steady rise in new housing units from the mid-'90's through 2007, this only brought us back to the levels of the 1970's. Just looking at raw numbers, and not taking into consideration any demographic changes, it is hard to see any evidence of a wave of over-building.

Now let's take this data on housing starts, and see how it equates to changes in population and birth rates. There has been another consistent force in the US economy and American society over the recent past that makes us the envy of other Western nations – we have a robust birth rate and experience a consistent increase in population.

Who knows why we are more fertile? Maybe it's because Americans are more religious than Europeans, with a tendency towards larger families. Or could it be all that sex on television and in the media the conservatives are always complaining about. Whatever the cause, we're producing a lot of babies.

Below is a chart of births in the US over this same period, 1959-2007.

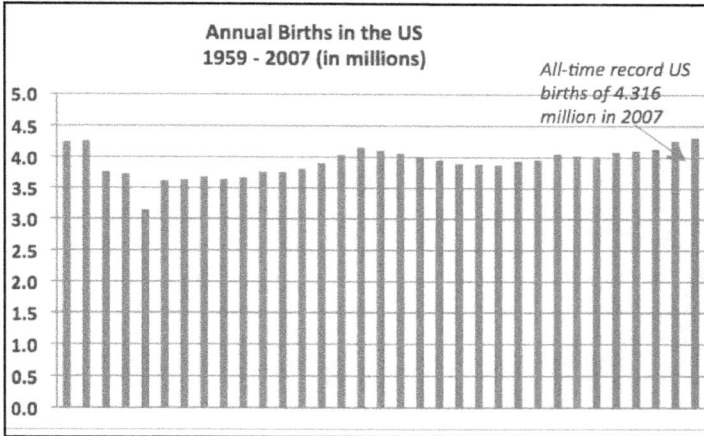

Figure 2: Source: US Census Department

As you can see from this chart, births - in absolute numbers - are actually now running above the highest levels of the baby boom era. The US is consistently generating more than four million births each year.

The combination of a steady birth rate, improvements in health and increases in life expectancy, and about one million legal immigrants every year has lead to an equally significant increase in population.[22]

22 Baseball purists argue that the old timers were better hitters than

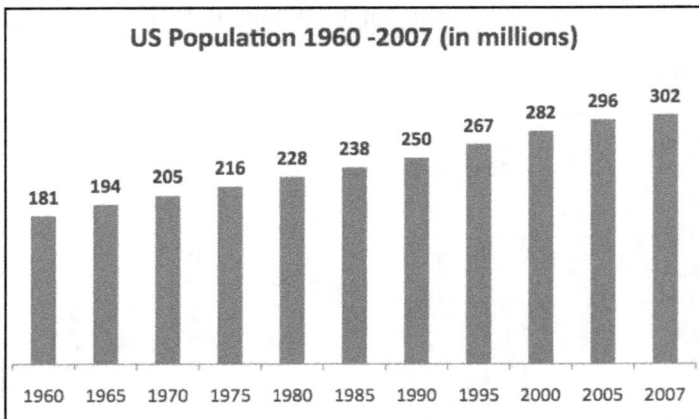

US Population 1960 -2007 (in millions)

Figure 3: Source: US Census Department

Now it's time to reassess housing rates in light of changes in demographics. First, here is a chart that shows the number of births each year per new housing unit.

modern ballplayers, due to the expansion of the major leagues and the ostensible dilution of pitching talent. But while the majors have doubled from 16 to 32 teams, the population has as well, so in percentage terms the same proportion of Americans play major league baseball as did in the 1950's. And the pool of available talent has more than doubled, as African-Americans and international players, particularly from Latin America, have entered the system in large numbers. That doesn't even begin to take into considerations other changes in the game, such as the rise of specialized relief pitchers (middle inning, late inning, closer) and improvements in baseball gloves (once barely larger than the hand they covered, now the size of a fruit basket). No, the hitters of today *are* better, just like swimmers and runners are faster.

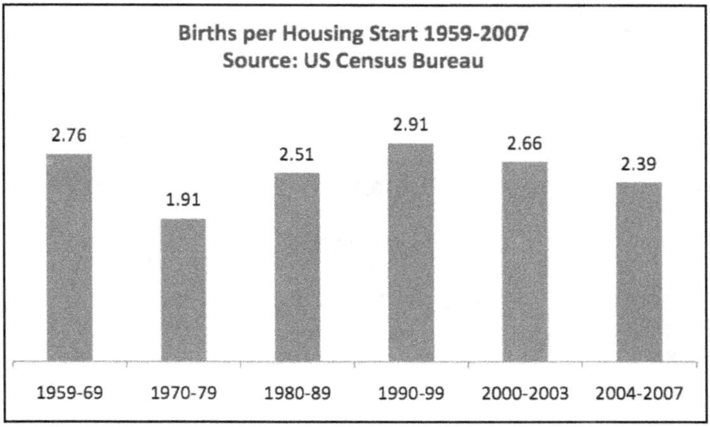

Figure 4: Source: US Census Department

Notice the interesting story this chart tells. The US has produced about one new house for every 2.5 births. The rate was a bit lower in the 1970's, and for this metric a lower number translates to a higher rate, in this case a new house for every 1.91 babies. I suspect there are some good reasons why housing construction may have picked up in the '70's. For one, the first baby boomers entered this decade in their mid-20's and exited it in their mid-30's, so there was a large demographic bulge that that was marrying and forming households at a higher rate. Also, most US cities went

-41-

through a major wave of violence in the 1960's and '70's. This was a time when the term "South Bronx" conveyed the most horrific urban blight imaginable, and when society began referring to "white flight" from the cities to suburbs. As people sought to move out of urban areas in large numbers, builders in the suburbs responded by constructing homes at a faster rate.

But notice the periods 2000-03 and 2004-07, again supposedly when we went through a wave of excess housing construction. Relative to birth rates, you can't find any evidence of overbuilding on the graph. In both four-year periods, the number of houses relative to the number of births was boringly consistent – right around the long-term average of 2.5.[23]

Here's another chart which presents a similar pattern, the rate of new construction relative to increases in the population, taking into account not only births but also immigration and mortality figures.

---

23 And I am boringly consistent, a fact which my family can readily attest to, as every night I have a popsicle from Trader Joe's for dessert. Every night. I rest my case.

**Increase in Population per Housing Start 1959-2007
Source: US Census Bureau**

			2.33	2.11	
1.77		1.49			1.75
	1.27				
1959-69	1970-79	1980-89	1990-99	2000-2003	2004-2007

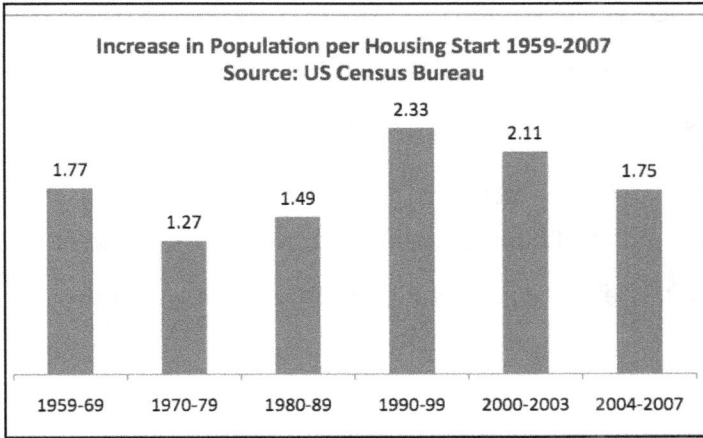

Figure 5: Source: US Census Department

As was the case when looking at birth rates, it's hard to find anything unusual about the relationship between construction and population growth when the housing bubble was supposedly underway. A reminder that lower numbers mean a higher rate. The 1970's, using this metric, were a period of higher construction, with one new housing unit per every 1.27 person increase in population. This higher rate was, not surprisingly, offset by a lower rate in the 1990's, with one new house per every 2.33 person increase in population.

Once again, as we look at the period when a housing bubble was supposed to be underway, we find the data is very consistent with the long-term averages.

There just is no evidence that construction accelerated during the housing bubble. Prices went up, but levels of construction stayed relatively steady.

Chapter 4: The Present: Construction Plummets

The past is a foreign country. They do things differently there.
L.P. Hartley

So we see that, contrary to popular belief, the housing bubble, which was certainly real, did not lead to a wave of excess construction. I also have made the case that markets generally work, and changes in price lead to changes in both demand and supply. So let's take a look at supply over the last few years. First look at the overall level of new home construction.

As you will see in the graph below, a sharp drop in construction activity has occurred. Foreclosures soared, the economy tanked, lenders stopped lending, and the leading culprit in the economic collapse was identified as the housing market. Not surprisingly, builders cut back sharply on their level of activity.

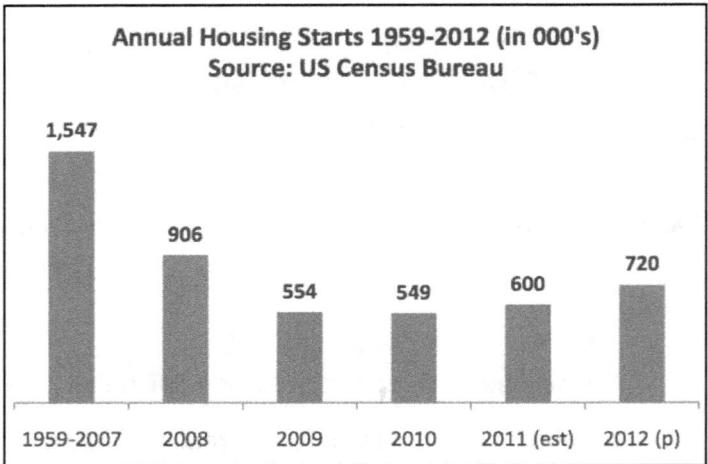

**Annual Housing Starts 1959-2012 (in 000's)
Source: US Census Bureau**

1,547 — 1959-2007
906 — 2008
554 — 2009
549 — 2010
600 — 2011 (est)
720 — 2012 (p)

Figure 6: Source: US Census Department

I believe an appropriate term for a drop of this magnitude might be "falling off a cliff." It is hard to overstate how dramatic this change is, and in fact when we adjust it for the annual loss in housing units, the drop will be even more precipitous. For nearly fifty years, housing starts were as steady the tides, averaging around 1.5 million units annually. As we've seen, the level of construction was, not surprisingly, closely correlated with changes in population and the birth rate. You'll see that I've included a projection for 2012 in this chart. As noted above, the lead time associated with building homes is substantial. Even if the market begins to recover immediately, it will take more than a year for construction rates to ramp up. You might say that for the purposes of this analysis, 2012 is already over. Any meaningful return to just historical construction rates, let alone an increase, is unlikely before 2013, and more realistically, perhaps not even until 2014.

The response of the builders to changing market conditions was exactly the opposite of conventional wisdom. Rates of construction stayed relatively consistent during the bubble years, but as the foreclosure crisis began to emerge, builders responded by turning off the spigot. It's possible that this was involuntary, and that it was the banks who shut off their funding. Maybe builders would have sustained their production if lenders had supported them. But either way, the system worked. Markets behaved the way that economic theory says they should.

The functioning of markets is often called into question, particularly in a crisis. Just as a fever is a sign that the body is fighting an infection, booms and busts are signs that markets are responding to imbalances. Recently, news reports are appearing that suggest that banks are becoming more flexible in dealing with foreclosures and distressed properties. Five years of their own pain and loss and finally gotten the banks to realize it is in their self-interest to deal rationally with borrowers who can't repay their loans.

One of the hallmarks of capitalism is that markets adapt to change. People have debated the morality of borrowers defaulting on loans, but in the end, a moral debate is irrelevant. A more flexible approach is emerging, not because banks have suddenly become more humane, but because it's good for business.

Now let's look at this data from a demographic perspective, starting again with births. Here is the birth rate over this period.

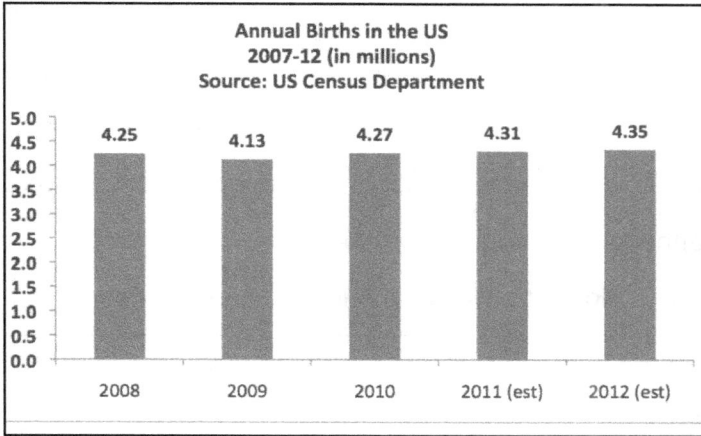

Annual Births in the US
2007-12 (in millions)
Source: US Census Department

Figure 7: Source: US Census Department

As the data shows, births are now running consistently above four million annually. Due to an overall
increase in population, the number of annual births is
now projected to be higher than during the baby boom.
We are at all time record levels. This is a cause for
celebration, not despair. A high birth rate demonstrates
confidence and belief in the future. Births are a key
driver of the economy, and in particular give a boost to
the housing market. As a parent myself, I can assure
you that nothing shrinks a house (or disposable

income) faster than the addition of a tiny baby. It's not the extra ten-pound person, it's the ton of stuff you buy to take care of them. If you are worried about the potential environmental impact, this data might concern you, although you would be wrong.[24]

Now let's look at the increase in population.

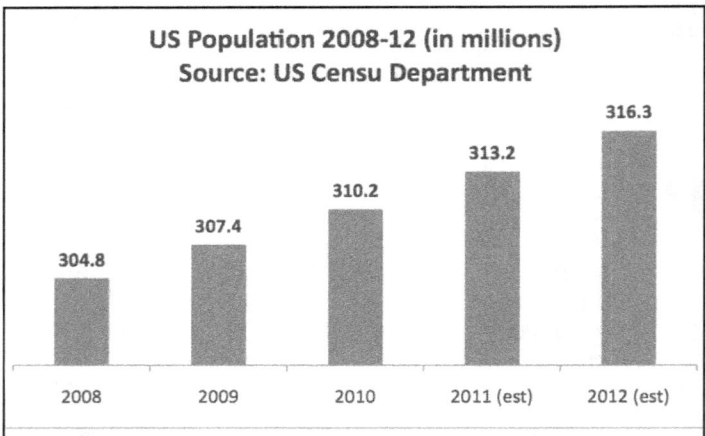

US Population 2008-12 (in millions)
Source: US Censu Department

304.8	307.4	310.2	313.2	316.3
2008	2009	2010	2011 (est)	2012 (est)

Figure 8: Source: US Census Department

Again, a consistent demographic pattern. The US remains in a period of steadily rising population. Each year the population grows about three million people, or around one percent.

---

24 Read *The Skeptical Environmentalist* by Bjorn Lomborg.

Over the last few hundred years, increases in population in Western nations have coincided with greater life expectancies, a higher material standard of living, improved sanitation and technology, a reduction in crime and violence[25], cleaner air and water, and advances in freedom and personal liberty, including the end of slavery, the emancipation of women, civil rights for blacks, and the end of the persecution of gays and lesbians. Notwithstanding all of this compelling evidence, there remain hysterical leftists who are convinced that disaster lurks just around the corner, just like it supposedly did in the 1960's and 1970's.[26]

But I digress. Back to the topic at hand. Here's a chart that shows housing starts relative to births.

---

25 See *The Better Angels of our Nature: Why Violence Has Declined*, by Steven Pinker.

26 Paul Ehrlich, in his 1968 doomsday prophecy, The Population Bomb, made a number of dire predictions, all of which failed to come true. He predicted massive waves of starvation due to food shortages, yet average global calorie consumption per capita has increased by 24% since his book was originally published. He predicted dramatic increases in global death rates, yet death rates have actually declined as life expectancies have increased around the world. The only recorded periods of widespread famine in modern times have occurred in non-democratic regimes, notably during in the Soviet Union in the 1930's and China in the 1960's. Astonishingly, despite being massively wrong, Ehrlich has maintained that his biggest mistake is that he was overly optimistic.

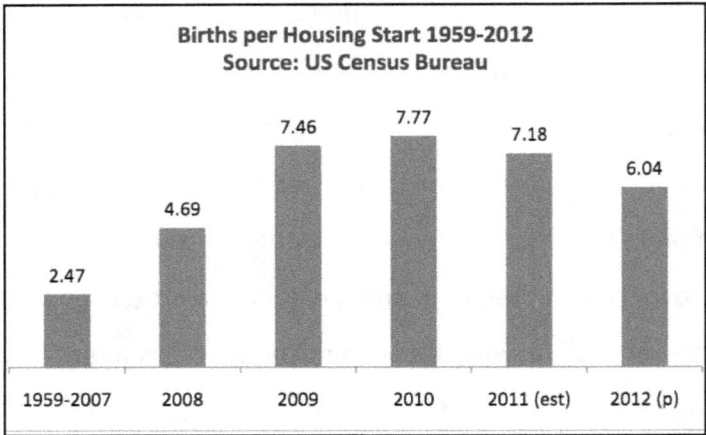

Figure 9: Source: US Census Department

Once again, the data is nothing short of startling. For fifty years, the US economy produced one new housing unit for every 2.5 babies, which sounds about right when you think about it. Now we at a third of that rate, and for five years running!

A similar pattern emerges when you examine housing starts compared to population growth.

Increase in Population per Housing Start 1959-2012
Source: US Census Bureau

5.35

5.22

4.77

4.26

3.08

1.68

| 1959-2007 | 2008 | 2009 | 2010 | 2011 (est) | 2012 (p) |

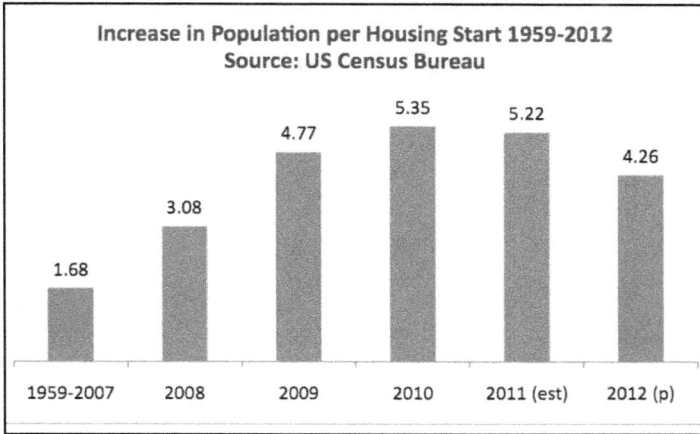

Figure 10: Source: US Census Department

I need to emphasize how absolutely amazing this data is. For fifty years, the US economy generated one new housing start per every 1.68 person increase in the population. More recently, that rate has declined by more than three times.

Housing construction contracted sharply once the housing bubble popped. This chapter has dealt with the gross number of new housing units only, not taking into account any housing units lost due to decay, conversion to other use or redevelopment. When we factor

in net growth, that is new units less units lost, the sheer
scale of the decline becomes even more dramatic.

Chapter 5: A Closer Look

By use you possess gain; by disuse you decline and lose.
Edwin Louis Cole

The US automotive industry sells close to fifteen million cars and light trucks annually. But the net increase in number of vehicles on the road each year is a much smaller number. Older cars are retired from service, junked for parts, recycled, or shipped to poorer countries. This is true for every durable good. For almost every new refrigerator rolling off a factory line, somewhere in America an old refrigerator is being thrown out.

This is an easy concept to understand in theory, but in practice can be hard to measure. The government keeps very accurate statistics about the rate of new residential housing construction. But figuring out how many housing units are lost to decay, abandonment or redevelopment is much trickier.

Let's start with a discussion of abandonment of housing units. During the brief period of time I worked in aviation finance, one of the strongest arguments in favor of the intrinsic value of aircraft is you can fly them somewhere else if necessary due to economic circumstances. If passenger traffic is weak in the US but growing in Asia, then you can redeploy aircraft to the stronger market. Or, if a carrier files for bankruptcy and liquidates, as Braniff, Eastern, Pan Am and TWA did, stronger carriers can pick up their fleet and – presto! – with a simple coat of paint, an airplane sporting the logo of a defunct company gets rebranded as American[27] or United.

So why might housing units get abandoned? The most obvious reason is the mobility of the population. Consider the following examples:

Since peaking in 1950, Detroit's population has declined by over 1.2 million people or 60%. Cleveland's population has declined by over 500,000, or more than half. St. Louis also shrank by over 500,000, about

27 As I write this, American is in bankruptcy as well and may be merged into another carrier.

two-thirds of its population. Philadelphia, 500,000, a quarter of its population. Pittsburgh, 400,000, more than half its population. Buffalo, over 300,000. Newark, nearly 200,000. Camden, 50,000. Baltimore, over 300,000.[28] Gary, Indiana has lost 100,000 residents, half its population. Youngstown, Ohio, 100,000, two-thirds of its population. Trenton, NJ, 40,000. Schenectady, 30,000. And on and on and on. It is probably a fair statement to say that just about every large and medium-sized city on the East Coast and in the Midwest that was a major center of manufacturing and industry in the early part of the 20th century has lost substantial population. Unlike airplanes, which can be flown to new locations, the housing units left behind were left to stay behind and rot.

The mobility of population within the US has

28 In 2008, my daughter started college as a freshman at MICA, an art school in Baltimore. We stayed in a suburban motel the night before move-in to student housing. Needing to stop at the pharmacy, and using GPS to find our way to campus, we were directed down a local arterial. Once we hit the periphery of downtown, we passed through a stretch of about thirty city blocks where virtually every single building was boarded up, scrawled with graffiti and abandoned. I had never seen such a wide swath of urban decay in my life. The neighborhood must have once contained a population in the tens of thousands, and was reduced to virtual obliteration, save for squatters living in the ruins.

been a powerful force in rural communities as well. One of the greatest developments in history as been the advance in farm productivity (and the primary reason why Ehrlich's predictions in The Population Bomb were so wrong). In Colonial times, 90 percent of the US population lived on farms. In the middle of the 19th century, the percentage declined to 70 percent. By 1900, it was down to 40 percent. By 1940, the figure reached 18 percent. By 1960, all the way down to 8.3 percent. 1970, 4.6 percent. Today, about 2 percent. And even though the overall population of the US has increased dramatically, in absolute numbers the farm population has declined from 30 million in 1940 to under 3 million today. Farmers and residents of agricultural communities moved, but left their houses behind.

The decline in farming population, which is a national phenomenon, is particularly acute in the Midwest. The US Census Bureau reported that from 1950 to 2007, the total population of the Midwest doubled, yet 244 out of 376 counties experienced population declines.

Another geographic shift in population was the

Great Migration, the exodus of African-Americans from the South in the first half of the 20th century. Although slavery had ended, it was replaced with Jim Crow, a system of segregation that kept blacks subject to pervasive discrimination, poverty and violence. As a result, a wave of blacks moved from the South in hope of a better life elsewhere. Historians estimate that over six million African-Americans were part of the Great Migration from the South to the North, Midwest and West. They too moved their bodies but not their homes.

Another factor that might contribute to loss of housing units is physical damage. FEMA reports damage from fires in number of units and dollars of loss, but does not indicate how many units are destroyed vs. the number that are damaged and subsequently repaired. But the data shows that about 350,000 – 400,000 residential fires have been reported over the past few years, with annual damages estimated at $6 - 8 billion.

The National Weather Service reports annual flood damages. The numbers, unlike fires, tend to fluctuate wildly, with damages in 1993 of $16 billion followed by damages in 1994 of $1 billion. The US Dept of Commerce estimates that since 1980, total losses from all catastrophic storms in the US amount to $750 billion.

Then there's redevelopment. Older homes or apartment buildings are often torn down for new construction, or converted to commercial use. Drive through just about any city or town and you'd find houses that have been converted to stores, restaurants, small offices or other businesses.[29]

According to the US Census Bureau, the total inventory of housing units in the US is 131 million. About one-third, or 41 million units, date from before 1959. Another 15 million were built during the 1960's. So, over 40% of the housing stock is fairly old. While it's true that a well-maintained home can survive for over a century, in general, it's likely that as homes ages they decline in value from a combination of wear and tear, undesirable location and outmoded design.

29 I once visited the headquarters of an online school in Ojai, California operating out of a three bedroom ranch house similar to the home I grew up in. I could picture myself fighting with my brother over which TV show to watch.

To summarize:

- Tens of millions of people moved away from farms and rural communities, which have experienced permanent population declines.

- Six million African-Americans migrated from the South. Large and medium- sized cities in the East and Midwest have lost millions in total population. Many major cities such as Cleveland, Detroit and St. Louis have permanently lost more than half their population.

- Fire causes billions of dollars of annual damage.

- Extreme weather causes billions of dollars of annual damage.

- Many housing units are lost due to development or conversion to commercial use.

- Tens of millions of housing units are extremely old.

My goal with this data is to figure out an annual average for how many housing units are lost in the US. HUD, the Department of Housing and Urban Development, released a study of changes in housing inventory over the period 2007-09[30] and reported the following:

- 491,000 units were lost to demolition or disaster

- 288,000 units were lost to non-residential use

- 302,000 units were lost to damage or condemned

- 400,000 units were lost in "other ways"

Using HUD estimates would indicate an annual loss rate of 370,000 units. The Census Bureau has estimated the annual loss rate at about 0.3%. With a total US housing inventory of 131 million units, that equates to an annual loss rate of 390,000.

Given that two government agencies, HUD and the Census Bureau, have estimates that are relatively close, for my analysis I assume that 375,000 housing units are lost annually for the current time period.

The loss of housing units needs to be taken into consideration as a rate, relative to the total US housing inventory. The data on housing inventory is shown below.

---

30 http://www.huduser.org/portal/periodicals/ResearchWorks/RW_september_11.html

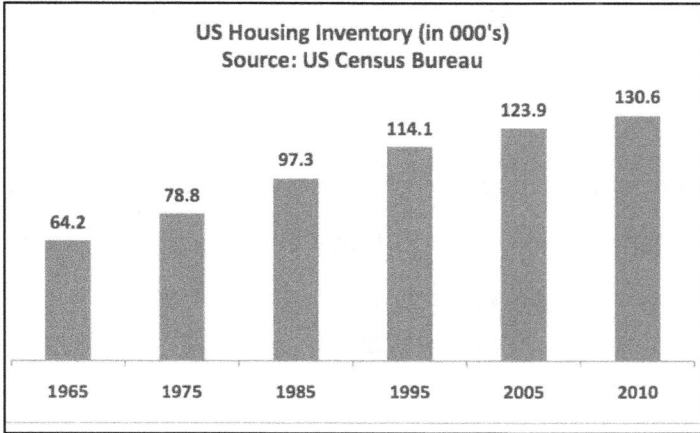

US Housing Inventory (in 000's)
Source: US Census Bureau

Year	Value
1965	64.2
1975	78.8
1985	97.3
1995	114.1
2005	123.9
2010	130.6

Figure 11: Source: US Census Department

As you can see, the total amount of housing inventory has about doubled, which is not surprising, as the population has approximately doubled over the same time period. Taking into account the increase in housing inventory, I have assumed the following loss rates for prior decades, when the total amount of housing was lower than it is today:

- 1960's: 200,000 units annually
- 1970's: 225,000 units annually
- 1980's: 275,000 units annually

- 1990's: 325,000 units annually
- 2000-07: 350,000 units annually

These annual assumed loss rates are consistent with the lower inventory for prior periods, rounded to the nearest 25,000 units. And, for periods from the year 2007 forward, I will use the 375,00 figure that is based Census Bureau and HUD research.

So, I will now present the data on construction activity from the last chapter, but this time taking into account annual losses in housing units. Here is the total amount of new construction, net of losses of units.

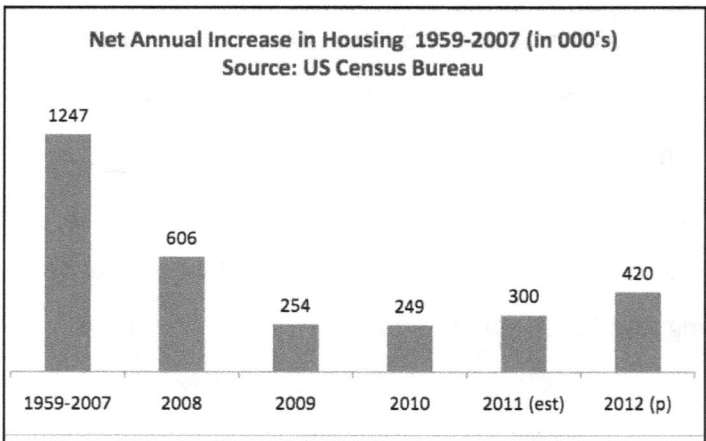

Figure 12: Source: US Census Department adjusted

As you can see, construction activity hasn't just declined, it's absolutely cratered. Rates are down 80%. Considering how stable this data has been for so long, the decline is extreme and unprecedented. And the data is also confirmation that markets work. In the face of declining prices, production of housing units screeched to a near-halt.

Next we'll examine housing growth relative to the birth rate.

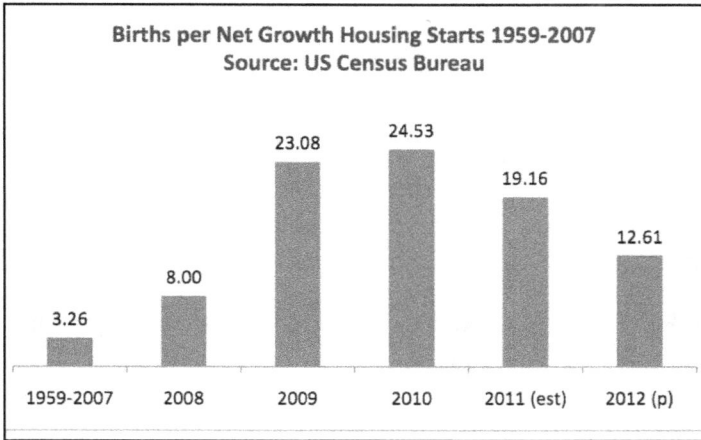

Figure 13: Source: US Census Department adjusted

Wow! For fifty years, the US added one net new housing unit per every 3.26 babies born. In 2008 and 2010 the economy added one net new house for every 23 and 24 babies, respectively.

Finally, let's look at net growth in housing relative to increase in population.

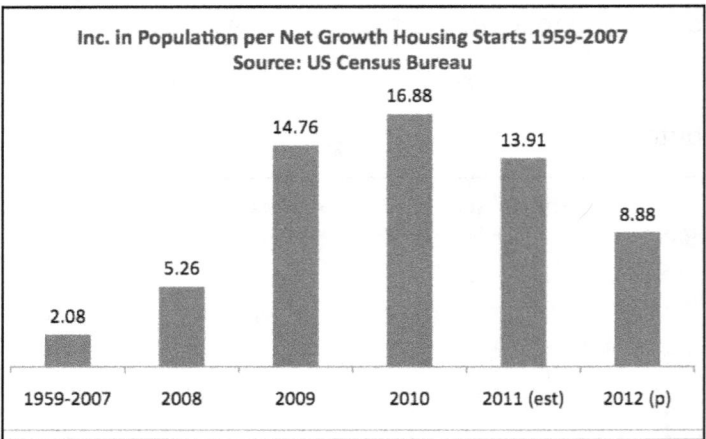

Inc. in Population per Net Growth Housing Starts 1959-2007
Source: US Census Bureau

1959-2007	2008	2009	2010	2011 (est)	2012 (p)
2.08	5.26	14.76	16.88	13.91	8.88

Figure 14: Source: US Census Department adjusted

Again, the decline relative to demographic data is staggering. From one net new housing unit per every two person increase in population to one net new unit every seventeen person increase.

Construction rates were relatively steady for fifty years. Nothing in the demographic data suggested that there was a period of overbuilding. What if the US economy had continued to produce new houses during 2008-2012[31] at the same rate as the prior fifty years? The charts below show this information. You can see what construction would have been ("Normal"), using the long term average of new homes relative to the population increase.

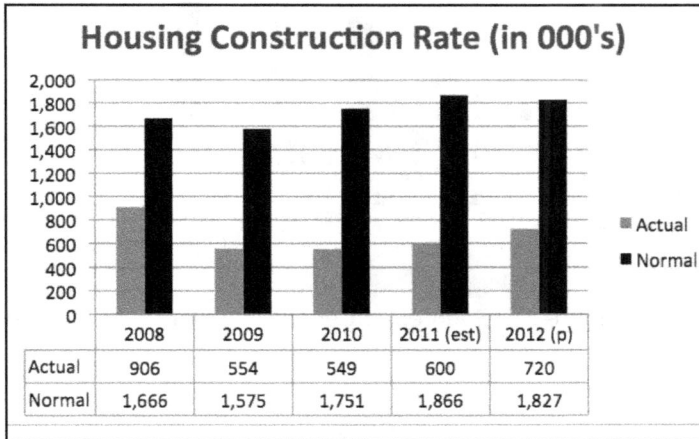

Housing Construction Rate (in 000's)

	2008	2009	2010	2011 (est)	2012 (p)
Actual	906	554	549	600	720
Normal	1,666	1,575	1,751	1,866	1,827

Figure 15: Source: US Census Department adjusted

31 Because of the long lead times associated with housing production, I am treating the construction estimate for 2012 as part of the historical time frame in this analysis. As a practical matter, ramping up production in 2012 materially beyond this number would require a concerted national effort equivalent to increasing armament production at the start of World War Two. It is simply not going to happen.

Here you can see the deficit in construction per year, on an annual and cumulative basis. Now let's look at the level of construction activity over the years since the housing crisis hit. Taking into account loss of units measuring net construction, the results are striking. A substantial shortage is developing.

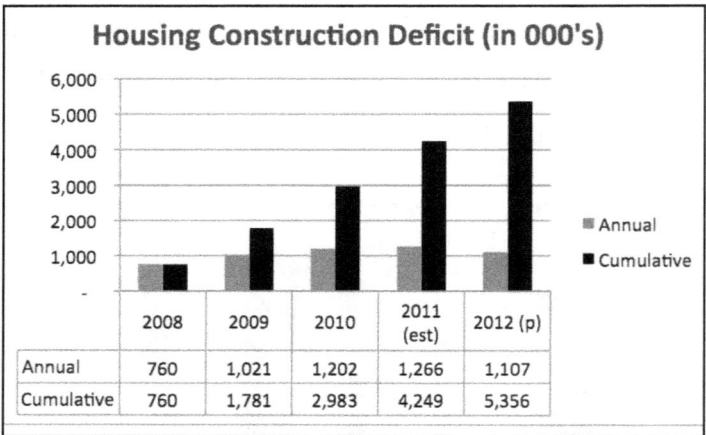

Housing Construction Deficit (in 000's)

	2008	2009	2010	2011 (est)	2012 (p)
Annual	760	1,021	1,202	1,266	1,107
Cumulative	760	1,781	2,983	4,249	5,356

Figure 16: Source: US Census Department adjusted

Over the period 2008-12, the cumulative shortage in housing construction was in excess of five million units (with a reminder that based on lead times associated with residential development, potential construction for 2012 is more or less fixed at this point). A total of five million homes that should have been built based on an increase in the population, weren't.

Chapter 6:
How Much is That Doggie in the Window?

In God we trust. All others bring data.

D. Edwards Deming

My analysis so far has consisted of relating construction activity to demographic data. This has been
instructive, but we are missing one key component: are
houses affordable? It's all well and good that there is a
shortage of housing units. The shortage, as logicians
like to say, is a necessary but insufficient condition for
a rebound in the market. What we need to know is not
merely whether there is a shortage, but if at current
price levels homes represent a good value.

Just looking at prices in absolute dollars in not nec-
essarily helpful. One also needs to factor in inflation and
the relationship between prices and average incomes.

Fortunately for the purposes of this analysis, the
hard work of calculating the relative prices of houses

has already been done for us. The National Association of Realtors publishes a statistic known as the "Housing Affordability Index." This measure compares the median income in the US to the median house price, taking into account interest rates to determine a monthly mortgage payment. When the index equals 100 exactly, it means that someone earning the median income can afford to purchase the median-priced home. Just a reminder on the difference between median and average. The median is the number that represents half the values above and half below. It is a better measure of a population when data is skewed in one direction. The price of a house cannot go below zero, but the upper limit in places like in Malibu is in the stratosphere. If you live in a town where ten ordinary houses are on the market for $250,000, and one rich guy's estate is being sold for $10 million, the median price of homes on the market would be exactly $250,000, while average price of a house for sale in your town would be $1.1 million. Because of this asymmetrical nature of housing prices (limited on the downside, virtually unlimited on the upside) using the median is a better reflection of what most people (except statisticians) would refer to as the average.

Let's summarize what we've covered so far. Housing construction remained relatively steady for nearly fifty years. Home prices soared in the early 2000's, propelled by speculative investment, lax lending standards and active encouragement by the US government to goose home ownership rates. Fannie Mae and Freddie Mac both were used by Congress as a social policy tool to put more people into homes, especially those with lower incomes who could not otherwise qualify for conventional mortgages. When buyers were presented with super-low teaser rates (exploding ARMS), they were reassured by unscrupulous mortgage brokers not to worry, because they would simply refinance at a higher value when it came time for the interest rate to explode, er, that is, reset.

When the crash came, it hit harder, perhaps harder than any economic collapse most people have seen in their lifetimes. When the Internet bubble popped, the damage was most heavily concentrated among technology companies, especially dotcoms. In fact, while technology centers like Silicon Valley and Seattle were struggling, home prices in South Florida were positively sizzling, creating a local boom where everyone was eager to get in on the next beachfront condo.

But the impact of the housing bubble has been much worse, because it literally has affected the entire country, including people who simply sat still and did nothing. If you owned a home during the last few years, it likely declined in value by at least one-third, regardless of where you live or whether you tried to refinance to use your equity as a source of cash. And, if you want to relocate, perhaps for a new job, to get an extra bedroom if you have a growing family, to downsize if you are an empty nester, or to retire to a new location, you've likely been stuck in place. Because even if you can buy a home for dramatically less than it would have cost a few years ago, you have suffered a similar decline in the home you already own. And if you have the bad luck to have bought a condo, or in a remote new development where construction activity froze in place, there may simply be no buyers for your property other than opportunistic investors, who are looking to pay pennies on the dollar.

But, because markets do in fact work, the forces that will propel an eventual recovery are now in place. A shortage of housing units is developing, and affordability is practically off the charts in terms of houses being cheap relative to incomes. Those reduced prices and mortgage rates below 4% mean that housing has never been a better bargain, as the chart below shows.

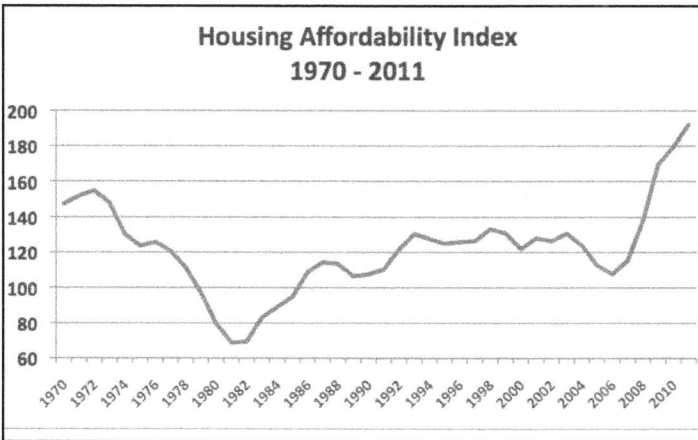

Housing Affordability Index
1970 - 2011

Figure 17: Source: National Association of Realtors

From an all-time low of 69.5 in 1982, back when mortgage rates were over 15%, affordability is now at record highs, at close to 200. As a reminder, when the index goes up, it means that housing costs are lower (relative to incomes). At 69.5, the median income in the US could afford to purchase a house at only 69.5% of the median home value. At a measure of 200, which is about the current level, the median income can purchase a home at double the national median price. Houses are three times cheaper than they were thirty years ago. Given the basic fundamental need for housing, and the size of the market, we are getting to a point where further large increases in affordability border on the inconceivable.

So, given all the above, what could go wrong? How might the recovery I predict be prevented, or slowed down by several years? After all, there are still plenty of prophets of doom out there predicting further huge declines ("massive waves of starvation") even thought the evidence does not support their claims. But, to be fair, nothing in life is certain.[32] The Titanic was unsinkable. Polaroid at $400 per share in the 1960's could only go higher. And so on.

So let's go through a list of possible factors that could make my prediction go awry. I'll divide them between two categories, the "known unknowns" and the "unknown unknowns." Allow me to explain the difference.

Known unknowns are factors that we know we will be able to measure in the future, such as the rate of unemployment or changes in GDP. We don't know what those rates will be, but we know the data will be available. Unknown unknowns are factors that are completely outside of any conventional probability analysis, such as the likelihood that a mad ayatollah will get his hands on a nuclear weapon and set off World War Three, which could result in the deaths of hundreds of millions and the return of the Western world back to the Stone Age.[33]

---

32 As Samuel Goldwyn said, "I hate making predictions, especially about the future."

33 The Saudi Arabian Oil Minister Sheik Yamani, said "The Stone Age didn't end because the world ran out of stones." It is in Saudi Arabia's interest for oil not to remain at permanently high prices, because that will simply accelerate consuming nations to invest in competing technologies.

So, let's start off with the unknown unknowns, which I will consolidate into a single category: unimaginable disaster (World War Three). As I contemplate this future, I am reminded of a job I had in a convenience store in New Jersey in the early 1980's, one of several that helped pay my way through college. It was terrible work at minimum wage, and involved, among other things, slicing cold cuts, a task which resulted one evening in accidentally cutting off enough flesh from my thumb to require a visit to the emergency room.[34]

This was during the early years of the Reagan administration, when tensions between the US and the Soviet Union seemed to be rising. At the time, there were a lot of people who believed in a "survivalist" way of life, which involved stocking up on canned food, securing access to a cave or other form of primitive shelter and in general taking precautions for when civilization would be reduced to rubble. One of the other employees in the convenience store, Charlie, was

[34] During that visit I noticed a young woman I recognized who worked in the deli department of the local supermarket coming in with a plastic bag of ice that I could only imagine contained a digit that needed to be reattached.

a big believer in this philosophy, and assumed that a nuclear holocaust was imminent (Since we were situated in central Jersey, located roughly midway between the two most likely strategic targets, New York City and Washington, D.C., presumably the odds of survival were negligible, but Charlie was not the type to be swayed by logic). He told me that he was maintaining a huge cache of pennies, as the value of the copper in one penny actually exceeded its monetary value of one cent. Once the bombs started to fly, Charlie informed me with a healthy dose of self-assurance, he would be sitting pretty with his valuable supply of copper.

However, to turn a profit on his investment, he would probably have to liquidate it by the ton. And to do so would require finding a working smelter, along with enough rudimentary aspects of a functioning economy, such as working roads, transportation equipment and a banking system. I had a mental image of Charlie, pushing a wheelbarrow filled with pennies across a smoldering, radioactive moonscape, wondering if he could find a copper smelting plant that had survived the attack.

So I think it's safe to ignore the unknown unknowns. Catastrophe is bad for everything, including houses and investments. Knowing that Armageddon is possible does little to inform this analysis. So let's turn our focus on the known unknowns. These are the types of things that fluctuate, but we just don't know what the outcomes will be. I'll review the main risks in detail.

1. Recession

Probably the biggest challenge to a housing recovery is the economy slipping back into recession. My crystal ball is as cloudy as everyone else's. I don't know what the economy will do in the future, but I have a hunch. Since the end of World War Two, there have been eleven official recessions, the definition of which is two consecutive quarters of a decline in economic output, or GDP. Recessions typically last for about a year, with several shorter than that, and a typical overall decline in GDP of around 2-4%. The recession we are just coming out of, which does not appear to have been a name that has caught on yet (The Bush Recession? The Obama Recession? The Great Recession?) was the most severe of any during the post-war period, lasting eighteen months, resulting in a 5.1% decline in GDP and an unemployment rate that peaked at 10.1%. And this recession either triggered, or was caused by, that darn housing crisis. While the downturn, as measured by GDP is officially over, it seems as much statistical fluke as genuine reality. Unemployment remains stubbornly high and GDP growth is positive but sluggish. If this is a recovery, it doesn't feel like it to a lot of people.

But consider another perspective. Think of recession as being analogous to illness for a generally healthy person. Occasionally you'll get sick, but your normal condition is feeling good. Same with the US economy. During the post-war period, the US economy has been in growth mode about 80% of the time. Recessions are not a normal state of affairs, growth is. Since March of 1991, at the end of the recession that doomed the presidency of George W. Bush ("Read my lips; no new taxes") and ushered in the if-it-feels-good-do-it Clinton era, the economy has been in growth mode more than eighteen years and in recession for a mere twenty-eight months.

The US is the world's most productive and dynamic economy. Even our colleges and universities are run like businesses, fielding professional sports teams that generate massive profits for everyone involved.[35] We have a culture that values risk taking and entrepreneurship. The right type of billionaire – such as Mark Zuckerberg or the late Steve Jobs – is widely admired. (The wrong type, such as a hedge fund manager, is viewed as an oppressor, in a great display of the meaning of cognitive dissonance). There even is an entire industry, venture capital, that provides funding to small startup companies in hopes of backing the next Google or Facebook.

Yes, the current recession has been nasty. But the economy is growing. As I write this, GDP has increased for seven consecutive quarters. The private sector is creating jobs, unemployment is coming down,

35 Except, alas, for the players, who are viewed as criminals if they accept any remuneration for their valuable services.

consumer spending is going up, and corporate profits are healthy. And as noted previously, our economy is also turbo-charged by a birth rate that other Western nations like Italy or Japan can only dream of. I think it's reasonable to assume that ten years from now, we'll have had a typical pattern of eight or nine years of growth, and only one or two of recession.

2. Foreclosures

You could probably characterize the wave of foreclosures as the biggest overall risk to a housing recovery. This is a topic that has received tremendous media attention.

But the important point is that the problem, while admittedly huge, is getting smaller. In December of 2011, the most recent data available as of the date of publication of this book, RealtyTrac reported that foreclosures of 224,394 represented a 14% year-over-year decline. This is the fifteenth consecutive month that foreclosures have declined year-over-year! For the third quarter of 2001, foreclosures were down

34% year-over-year. In August of 2011, RealtyTrac reported that foreclosures had declined to a forty-four month low.

Another reason why foreclosures are less of a risk to a housing recovery is that they are heavily concentrated in just four states: California, Nevada, Arizona and Florida. House prices have declined just about everywhere, but waves of foreclosures have not been an issue in every market.

We should assume that the foreclosure rate will continue to decline over the next few years, another example of the self-correcting power of free markets. First of all, lending standards have tightened significantly since the crash (another risk factor, to be discussed below). The days of the "liar loan" are over.[36] Anyone who has bought a home in the last few years has almost certainly been subject to an appropriately thorough review of their income and their ability to

---

36 In an article that highlighted the excesses of the market at the height (or depth) of its insanity, a major newspaper profiled a man who claimed he earned $100,000 as a Mexican folk singer, and he included a photograph of himself wearing a sombrero as part of his application to document his income.

service their mortgage. So the overall credit quality of applicants has improved since the housing bubble.

Also, as discussed above, the economy, while sluggish, is growing. Over seven million jobs were lost during the (Bush? Obama?) recession, which certainly contributed to the default rate. Even in normal times, there will always be some percentage of borrowers who suffer personal financial distress and cannot make their mortgage payment, so the foreclosure rate will never be zero. Now that the economy is back in (moderate) growth mode, this one-time massive loss in jobs is most likely now behind us.

Also, "strategic" foreclosures, i.e., decisions to walk away from onerous mortgages that amount to throwing good money after bad, are probably winding down, since anyone who is likely to find this a financially advantageous move has probably done so already at some point over the past four years. During the Internet bubble, I remember talking with a colleague at the time about some of the crazy job offers that were floating around (unfortunately, none came my way). He commented that it was a good idea to be loyal to your employer, but not to the point of stupidity. If someone offers to double your pay, you shouldn't, as he put it, "turn off your brain." Similarly, if you bought a house in declining market with an "exploding" option-ARM, and you are holding an $800,000 mortgage for a property that is now worth only $400,000, you would have to similarly be an idiot for continuing to make those monthly payments.[37] And the rules only make it worse. Lenders have generally resisted efforts to reduce principal and have been extremely uncooperative and inefficient in administering programs to reduce interest payments. Even if you can refinance, repaying a loan in full for a property worth 50% of the principal amount is in fact stupid. Especially if you bought the house with no or almost no money down.

But now that home prices have dropped so dramatically, keeping current on one's mortgage pay-

---

[37] Note the inherent unfairness of the bankruptcy code. Corporate giants like GM can take themselves into bankruptcy to void contracts, get out of debt obligations, and force their unionized employees to absorb pay cuts and pension reductions. This is regarded as good business. When an individual tries to do the same in their personal life, it is considered morally reprehensible.

ments is less of a big deal. If you bought a house for $300,000 within the last few years, you probably put 10%-20% down. If you think it's now only worth $250,000, and you need a roof over your head anyway, you probably wouldn't walk away from a down payment of $30,000-$60,000 and take a major hit to your credit rating. You would do what any sensible person from my parents' generation would have done – ignore the short-term fluctuations in the value of your home and get on with the business of living your life. And then, twenty or so years down the road, when the kids are raised, you'll have paid down most of your mortgage and be sitting on a valuable asset that you can either live in at a permanently low cost, or sell and use as a springboard to finance a move somewhere else.[38]

Finally, a significant percentage of foreclosures are being purchased by investors and converted to rentals. Again, this is an example of how markets work. *The New York Times* recently reported

[38] In the case of my parents' generation, that would be Florida. Most people are unaware that during the 1970's a law was passed in several Northeastern states requiring Jews to relocate to within one hundred miles of Miami by their seventieth birthday.

that some students attending University of California-Merced are going into shared rentals in a subdivision filled with foreclosed McMansions. And, amazingly, while enjoying luxury features such as Jacuzzi tubs, walk-in closets and Great Rooms (which are great for parties), they actually pay about 50% less than the cost of boxy, cramped on-campus dorms. And the university's free bus system provides service to subdivisions with heavy concentrations of students. One neighbor, struggling to pay his mortgage for a house purchased for $532,000 and now worth $221,000 remarked these were "the luckiest students" he'd ever seen.

The foreclosure issue for condos is even less of a challenge. Condos take a few years to build, and when they are completed, an entire building comes on the market at once. And, it's likely that most markets have multiple projects underway, so the problems at any single building are compounded by all the other new developments completed at the same time. But the good news, in terms of market impact, is that condos are financed by institutional investors, because a single project can cost as much as $200-$300 million, and all the money has to be spent on construction before the units can be sold. That level of funding takes sophisticated lenders, the same type of sharp business people who take a company through bankruptcy to reduce costs. When a condo project has $300 million of construction spending sunk into it, but the market value is only $150 million at completion, either the developer files for bankruptcy or the lenders seize the property directly. They'll convert the project to a rental, or refinance the project at its new value, and sell the units at sharply lower prices.

A couple of examples. In September of 2010, the South Beach, Miami market had an 18-year (year!) supply of unsold condos, as 5,100 units of new inventory had been added in forty-seven different projects. Over two thousand units were on the market, and the sales rate for the third quarter was a grand total of nineteen units.

Now, fast forward to September 2011, just one year later. The unsold supply of units was below one hundred. The market cleared in just one year, because lenders seized properties and either converted them to rentals or slashed prices.

Or consider my hometown, Bellevue, Washington, where a considerable amount of inventory also came on the market. One major project, part of a mixed-use development including office space and luxury retail, and containing over four hundred condos in two towers, was converted to rentals. Just like that, over $200 million of unsold condos disappeared from the market. A few blocks away, an even larger project of over five hundred units, consisting of two towers, one forty-two stories tall, and the other forty-three stories, a scale of construction comparable to Manhattan, was seized by lenders in January 2011, with about eighty percent of the units unsold. The remaining units have had their prices cut by about forty percent, aligning them with the new lower market pricing. Nearly one thousand unsold condos in just two projects created a massive over-supply in a medium-sized market in mid-2010. In the space of six months, problem solved.

This is not to suggest that foreclosures are not a significant problem, because they are. But the foreclosure crisis will heal itself with the passage of time. And during that time, foreclosed homes will comprise a smaller and smaller percentage of total inventory for sale.

3. Lenders Won't Lend

This is another potential risk for a recovery, that too many borrowers are shut out of the market. Mortgage rates are at all-time lows, below 4%. But the hitch is that you have to qualify. Not enough people can take advantage of low rates to fuel a recovery in the housing market, or so the argument goes.

Another way to think about the issue is that lenders have returned to more prudent business practices. Back when I bought my first house, in 1988[39], you either put 20% down or faced a much higher borrowing cost. Oh, and mortgage rates were around 14%, a reduction from the nearly 20% level of rates that was a major

39 At the time I had a full head of hair and have photographic evidence to prove it; nonetheless, my children believe I was born fully-formed as a grouchy adult. In Yiddish, someone with my personality type is known as *nudge* (note it does not rhyme with budge).

factor in Jimmy Carter being a one-term president.

Mortgages lenders make loans for a very simple reason: it's a business. When they lend successfully, they make a profit. They have an incentive to lend money with an appropriate balance between risk and reward. During the bubble, the perception of risk was skewed, and also fraud was prevalent. It's likely the pendulum has now swung too far in the other direction. Yet I managed to refinance during 2011, taking advantage of low rates. Funding is definitely available for qualified buyers. And lower prices also help the market recover. Coming up with a 20% down payment on a $200,000 house might be difficult, but it's not inconceivable. Getting in the habit of saving up for a down payment might not be a bad type of old fashioned value to revive.[40]

4. Owning a Home is Passé

Once upon a time, for a man in the United States to be considered well-dressed, he had to wear a hat

[40] Not all old fashioned values are virtuous. It used to be okay to discriminate against gays, blacks, women and Jews.

(think *Mad Men*). Then, the most stylish and sexy president and first lady, JFK and Jackie, captured America's hearts. Kennedy was the first president in memory who did not wear a hat during his inauguration. Suddenly, despite over a century of fashion history, hats were so last week, and quickly went out of style. Today all we have left is the phenomenon of wearing a baseball cap backwards, or even worse, sideways. Oh, the inhumanity![41]

Could owning a house go the way of hats? No, it can't.

Nothing is more basic and fundamental to human nature than a sense of home. Go back to any archeological dig, and you find evidence that people have been living in homes for as long as we have been around as a species. It is a basic attribute of being human.

41 I cover my head with a hat year-round, for many years with a baseball style cap (facing forwards, thank you!) and more recently a beret that my long-suffering wife urges me to wear backwards, a la Samuel L. Jackson. I mentioned to a colleague of mine once that I wore it because my parents, who live in Florida, are concerned about skin cancer, and told me that I had to wear a hat, even in the Seattle climate, to protect myself, given that I am fair-skinned and bald. My colleague thought I covered my head because I was Jewish. That he would have understood. But he was astonished by the tradition of listening to one's parents like a good Jewish boy, even into one's fifties.

You might recall that a few years ago a similar argument, albeit in a smaller way, was being made against carbohydrates, this despite the fact that the most basic of Christian prayers is for one's daily bread. Carbohydrate-related stocks like Panera Bread plunged in value. The movement petered out, and we returned to the diet that we've been eating for millennia. So too with houses.

Everyone needs a roof over their head, but that doesn't mean it can't be a rental. The argument that it is advantageous to rent can be true for some people for extremely sensible reasons. Certainly some percentage of the population is better off renting, especially people who value flexibility in their personal life and don't want to have a chunk of their net worth tied up in a long-term and illiquid investment.

But that percentage is at most somewhere around 35-40% of the population. Even people who value flexibility also like a backyard, or simply to be king or queen of their castle. Again, returning to my youth, I recall that it was a common dream among those starting their careers to eventually own a home and be free of the hassle of a landlord. In one of the crummy apartments my wife and I lived in during our college years, we awoke one year on Yom Kippur morning, the holiest day on the Jewish calendar, because a maintenance man with a security key let himself in to do "an inspection." Some months earlier we had complained to our landlord about various items needing repair, such as an exterior wooden staircase with railings that swayed wildly, was installed half-painted (half of each step, not half the steps) and was not anchored to the ground, so it wobbled as you walked on it.

This was the seamier side of New Jersey and in a town that had rent control[42], so it probably was an extreme example. But there is a sense of satisfaction to being an owner, provided you can afford it. You don't need to ask permission to paint a wall or use a nail to hang a picture.

And finally there is the affordability issue. As noted earlier, relative to incomes, homes have never

42 Rent control laws are inspired by good motives but have negative consequences because owners of rental property become unwilling to invest in their maintenance and upkeep. Like most government interference in the free market, good intentions produce bad outcomes.

been this cheap. At some point, prices becomes so compelling that they tilt the balance. If you are a first-time buyer in today's market, and prices are 30-60% lower than a few years ago, the opportunity is very enticing.

5. The Data is Unreliable

This might be the strongest argument against a recovery. Over the past few years, so many millions of homes have been lost to foreclosure that this phenomenon has overwhelmed the system. There have been horror stories of people being foreclosed on where lenders have been unable to provide proof showing they hold the mortgage, or where those mortgage documents have been fraudulently prepared. The real estate industry is set up to track normal levels of activity, and the foreclosure wave has been anything but normal. In fact, in December 2011, the National Association of Realtors revised downward sales figures since 2007 for previously owned home because its methodology was not well-suited to track "for sale by owner" and bank owned properties.

But while this revision changes the level of the graph, it doesn't change the overall trend. And new construction remains relatively easy to track, because it is based on building permits, which is a reliable source of information. With affordability at record levels and construction down five years running, the fundamental components of this argument remain unchanged.

6. Europe is Teetering and Will Take the Global Economy Down With It

To me, Greece once represented backpacker paradise. In 1976 and '77, as I traveled around Europe on a shoestring budget, I mentally ranked the backpacker nations of the world as follows: Northern Europe was the most expensive, Italy was cheap compared to its Northern neighbors, Greece was cheap compared to Italy, Turkey was cheap compared to Greece, and everything East of Turkey – Afghanistan, Pakistan, India, etc., was so dirt cheap that room and board for a smelly hippie ran under $1 per day, not a lot of money even back then.

I recall staying in a private hostel in Athens for about 95 cents, and eating gyros for lunch and dinner at less than 20 cents apiece. Who could have imagined that in late 2011, a country known for beaches and tourism would threaten to drag down the global economy?

I married a Dutch woman in 1978 and spent about a year living in Holland. At the time, I marveled at the generous Dutch welfare system. In the US, if you lost your job and had a run of bad luck, you could find yourself living beneath a freeway overpass. In Holland, you would collect unemployment insurance equal to 90% of your last pay, most likely would be living in subsidized housing, and would have access to free health care. To me, as a naïve youth, it seemed that countries could choose to either be generous or stingy. Europe chose generosity, the US a social safety net that tears easily.

If only it were so simple. What Europe did choose was to fund a level of government spending that has proved to be unsustainable. There is a saying in economics: things go on until they can't. The capital markets have raised borrowing costs sky-high for the weakest of the European economies – Greece, Spain and Italy – and in early 2012 most of Western Europe was downgraded by S&P.

So, what can't go on, won't go on. European governments will have to decrease their level of debt. Some nations may drop out of the Euro zone.[43] But Europe still remains the world's largest economic region. Even if growth is sluggish, Europe is not going to collapse. Growth may be moderate for the next few years. On the other hand, this may be an opportunity for a return to the free market policies of Margaret Thatcher and Ronald Reagan of the 1980's. As Germans are increasingly asking themselves, why do we have to provide the funding so that Greeks can retire with full pensions at age fifty-five?

The world is full of risks. I'm sure the list in this chapter could be expanded, because life is uncertain. But the odds favor a recovery.

---

43 For Greece, that might be a positive development, as devaluing their currency would boost tourism.

Chapter 7: Trust Your Gut

Intuition is the source of scientific knowledge.

Aristotle

I am not an investment genius, far from it. But I have been right a couple of times in a major way. I remember in March of 2009, when it seemed the world was just about coming to an end, I walked by a television in our house as it was displaying the stock market news and saw that the Dow Jones Industrial Average was down to 6,500, a drop of about 60% from its all-time high in 2007. And, unlike the Internet bubble, when dotcoms with no earnings reached zany valuations, during the more recent bull market, valuation multiples were consistent with long-term averages, and unprofitable companies run by CEOs in their twenties were no longer Wall Street darlings. I did some quick research and saw that blue chip companies with highly profitable operations and tons of cash on their balance sheets, such as Microsoft and Disney, were trading at valuation of four times cash flow and price/earnings ratios in the single digits, both of which are extremely low levels on an historical basis. I said to myself this is ridiculous – there is absolutely no risk in the market when the planet's strongest and most well-managed companies are trading at these levels. What is Microsoft going to go down to? Three times cash flow? Two times? When a normal cash flow multiple would be more like 7-10, and a price/earnings ratio of 12-15?

I viewed stock prices at these levels as being the equivalent of the "unknown unknowns" I discussed in the previous chapter. The stock market wasn't just pricing in a recession, it was anticipating the collapse of Western capitalism. Maybe my old deli-slicing colleague with the wheelbarrow full of pennies would finally have his day in the sun.

But, I decided, the world had not come to an end, the pundits notwithstanding. I figured it was unlikely I would soon be sporting an animal pelt and hunting small game with a slingshot (although I regularly work out, I have the kind of figure that does not look well in a stone age garment, as from the waist down I am both skinny and bowlegged).

So I started buying stocks. My typical routine was (and still is) to get up early, eat a bowl of high fiber breakfast cereal washed down with a refreshing glass of prune juice, followed by a furious workout on the treadmill downstairs in front of the TV. I put the incline level to 6.5 degrees, strap on ankle weights and run with three-pound hand weights, ultimately working up such a copious amount of perspiration that I begin to generate my own micro-climate (warm and muggy). Oh, and I usually watch CNBC, the stock market channel. In those first few months after I began buying stocks, as the Dow rallied into the 7,000's and then the 8,000's, most commentators would emit a low, mournful chuckle, and explain that it was foolish to consider this a rally (notwithstanding that by definition a rise in stock prices *is* a rally), as the market was going to take another violent lurch downward taking stocks to levels one could barely imagine in their worst nightmare. They had the same view of someone buying stocks as you might take of a handicapped child struggling with a task beyond their capacity, saddened by the misery that people can be subjected to.

And then a funny thing happened. Stocks kept on going up, to the 9,000's, back above 10,000 and more recently trading above 12,000. Anyone who listened to the experts and stayed on the sidelines missed perhaps the greatest stock market rally they'll see in their lifetime.

After all of the analysis laid out above, I have a similar gut feeling today. Life remains normal. Overweight people in sweatpants continue to buy junk at the mall they don't need. They drive there in SUVs that are bigger than the Apollo 11 lunar landing module, and on the way home eat dinners at a chain restaurant containing 300% of the recommended daily caloric intake. Then they go home, switch on their one-hundred inch LCD TV, and half watch Jersey Shore or American Idol while they go online with their laptop, smart phone or iPad.

Yes, it's pretty unfortunate[44] that unemployment

44 I try to encourage my kids not to use the term "it sucks."

is still close to 10%. But the reverse of that is that the employment rate is over 90%, and those in the employed category have begun to loosen their purse strings and spent, if not like 1999, at least not like 2009, either. The Christmas season of 2011 just ended exceeded expectations, with online sales particularly robust.

And I keep on coming back to the numbers, which inform and reinforce my gut. The affordability index is at a forty-year high. Just to take an anecdotal example, in the bedroom community I grew up in, Kendall Park, NJ, with highly rated schools and in a township, South Brunswick, which *Money Magazine* recently rated as one of the ten best places in the country, three bedroom, two-bath homes on a third of an acre are listed for sale at $275,000. Yes, its 1960's construction, and these homes probably are in need of some serious updating. But with a 20% down payment, the monthly mortgage payment is around $1,000. Given the cost of renting, prices this low probably pencil out as an investment or even, given the lot size and school district quality, as a tear-down.

Finally, rental rates have been rising nationally, indicating a strong pent-up demand for housing. The brain and the gut are lining up for this.

Chapter 8:
Would You Buy a Used Car from This Guy?

A man who serves as his own lawyer has a fool for a client.
Common folk saying

I am going to start this chapter with a couple of caveats. I am not a registered investment advisor. I don't hold any type of securities license or have clients who pay me for investment recommendations. Therefore, if you follow my advice and lose money, it's your own fault. I'm just sharing my opinion, but there is a good chance I could be wrong, for a lot of reasons, including the fact I have been wrong a lot many times in the past.

Okay, I hope that provides me with sufficient legal ammunition in case someone comes after me with a lawsuit after following my advice.[45] With those

45 The prospectus for the initial public offering, or IPO, for LinkedIn, which is typical for this type of deal, included a list of risk factors that runs for over five pages, including the following:
• We have a short operating history in a new and unproven market, which makes it difficult to evaluate our future prospects and may

caveats out of the way, I'd like to point out that I believe that home building stocks represent a good, although clearly speculative investment opportunity. While home prices are down by 40-50%, the stocks of the major publicly traded builders are in some cases down even more.[46] Any decision to invest in the market depends on your own personal circumstances. And even if you have money to invest and can absorb a loss, you should still diversify. But if you have some capital you can take a bit of a risk with, I think the major home builders represent a compelling opportunity.

You can buy home builder stocks directly. Some of the largest include DR Horton (ticker symbol DHI) Lennar (LEN), KB Homes (KBH), Pulte Homes (PHM), Toll Brothers and Meritage Homes (MTH). Smaller, much more speculative builders include Beazer Homes

increase the risk that we will not be successful.
• If we fail to effectively manage our growth, our business and operating results could be harmed.
• We may invest or spend the proceeds of this offering in ways with which you may not agree or in ways which may not yield a return.
In other words, we might mess up and you could lose money, and if you do and try to sue us, don't tell us you weren't warned.
46 During the period that I wrote this book, Dec. 2011 – Feb. 2012, home builder stocks began to rally. Sorry I did not get this published sooner, as the investment opportunity was even more compelling only a couple of months ago.

(BZH), Hovnanian (HOV) and Standard Pacific (SPF).

Another perhaps more diversified way to invest in the sector is through one of two exchange traded funds (ETFs) that track the residential home sector. The first is the iShares US Home Construction index (ticker symbol ITB). This fund is designed to match the performance of companies that build homes, including mobile homes, although it includes related companies such as Home Depot and Lowes. The other ETF that covers this sector the SPDR Series Homebuilder Index (ticker symbol XHB). This index is also includes companies that participate broadly in the home market, including names such as Home Depot, Lowes and Bed Bath and Beyond, in addition to home builders.

In a recovery, home builder stocks are likely to outperform the overall real estate market. The market for previously owned homes is going to have a heavier-than-usual percentage for foreclosed and distressed properties for the next few years. These homes are not only less likely to be well-maintained, they also are a paperwork and bureaucratic challenge. I remember in 2010 I was chatting with a local investment banker involved in a deal I was working on, who mentioned he had just bought a foreclosed home in the Tacoma area, about an hour south of Seattle. He said the savings outweighed the hassle. At our next meeting, he got a call on his cell phone and said he had to leave immediately to drive straight to the courthouse, as he just learned that his lender was mistakenly foreclosing on *him*, not realizing it was the previous owner who ran into trouble and that he was current on his payments.

Another example. Just down the block from me, there is a house with a "Sold" sign on it that has been sitting empty for about four months. I asked a neighbor what was happening with the house and she said, "Everything takes longer when the bank is involved."

If you buy from the builder, you don't have to put up with any of this type of hassle. Closing is quick and predictable. The house by definition is brand new, so you don't have to worry that the last tenant took out his frustration on the property. And, any features that are desirable among current buyers will be included, such as modern floor plans, walk-in closets, etc. Finally, a lot of foreclosed homes are in places that no one wants to live. They are located in subdivisions with lots of other properties that are either empty or themselves suffering from neglect.

For all of these reasons, I expect that as the housing market recovers, builders will have a competitive advantage relative to foreclosures. Also, since construction rates need to triple from current levels to get back to normal, in a recovery they are going to be busy.

Chapter 9: A Prediction for the Future

The groundhog is like most other prophets; it delivers its prediction and then disappears.

Bill Vaughan

I predict that housing prices will stop declining in 2012, and may go up 1-3%. Then, starting in 2012, I anticipate prices rising by 5-8% per year for the next few years. Five years from now, in early 2017, I expect that prices will have risen about 40% from current levels.

This may seem to you like the peyote talking. But let's take a simple mathematical example. To make the calculation easy, assume the average price of a house was $100,000 at the peak. Prices nationally declined by one-third, or down to $67,000. If prices then rise by 33%, they will only go back up $89,000, which would still be an 11% decline from all time highs.

The math is even more extreme in depressed markets, like certain areas of California, Florida, Arizona or Nevada. Imagine a subdivision in one of those states where prices dropped by 60%. Again, to make the math simple, imagine that prices at their high were $100,000, and dropped by 60% to $40,000. A 60% increase would take the price only back up to $64,000, or still nearly 36% below peak prices.

Right now housing affordability is at an all time high of about 200, using the index developed by NAR. Assume we return to a period of more normal growth. If incomes go up by 3-4% over the next few years, which would be reasonable in a moderate recovery, then even with a 40% price rise, the affordability index would still be in a very favorable range.

Now let's talk about two other factors. The first is inflation. The Federal Reserve and the nasty recession have combined to keep inflation down to low single digits. If we have any pickup at all in inflation, just even to a rate of around 3-4%, real estate is an excellent hedge.

The other factor is emotion. I know a hedge fund manager who specialized in small cap stocks (the type of companies you've barely heard of, unlike giants such as IBM, Coca-Cola or Johnson & Johnson). He said that in the small cap world, stocks could go from "chic to geek" and vice versa almost overnight. Because these were small, speculative companies, they traded on emotion as much as detailed financial analysis.

Ah, emotion, what is sometimes referred to as "animal spirits." Humans have two brains, one in their head and one in their gut. Ultimately, emotions are a more powerful force than logic (in singles ads people may claim they are seeking out potential mates who enjoy yoga and the music of Cold Play, but they fall in love in spite of themselves over a smile, a way of tilting one's head, the sound of a person's voice (and find themselves forced to attend NASCAR and listen to country and western music for the rest of their lives).

At some point, even if I'm wrong about the timing, eventually housing prices will recover. With affordability at record highs, and mortgage rates at record lows, all it will take is a few months of news reports of prices going up and buyers snagging great deals for people to get motivated. The belief that real estate, or any asset, will rise in price can become a self-fulfilling prophecy.

Chapter 10: Markets Work

And it came to pass, that Pharaoh dreamed: and, behold, he stood by the river and, behold, there came up out of the river seven cows, well-favoured and fat; and they fed in the grass. And, behold, seven other cows came up after them out of the river, ill favoured and lean; and stood by the other cows upon the brink of the river. And the ill-favoured and lean cows did eat up the seven well-favoured and fat cows. And Joseph said unto Pharaoh: The seven good cows are seven years. And the seven lean and ill-favoured cows that came up after them are seven years they shall be seven years of famine.

Genesis, Chapter 43

One of my favorite authors is the neuroscientist Steven Pinker. In his book *The Blank Slate,* Pinker discusses how so much of the radical ideas of the 1960's and 1970's were flat-out wrong. Psychologists, sociologists and liberals of all types argued that categories such as gender were cultural artifacts. Biology was not destiny. There is no basic human nature, and

even categories like gender were simply cultural con-
structions. Anyone who claimed otherwise had to be
either sexist, racist, or a Nazi. Sometimes, this was
argued in reverse: if you claimed that blacks and whites,
or Westerners and inhabitants of the third world were
all fundamentally alike, that was racist as well.

Pinker completely demolishes this argument,
and I highly recommend this book to any curious reader. Take for example, the belief that children are overly
sexualized because of popular culture. But, culture
doesn't just exist floating out in space. It is a human
artifact, created by humans to fulfill human needs.
Anyone alive today is only here because they are
descended from ancestors who were successful at
sexual reproduction. It's not "culture" or "the media"
or some other force that is a feature of the universe
that is influencing the "blank slate" of humanity to be
interested in sex. It's the other way around: people that
are interested in sex and think about it a lot create a
culture where sex is a prominent feature.

Pinker describes that our brains and bodies have

been shaped by evolution to have certain innate traits. For example, learning to read and write is hard, but learning to recognize faces is effortless. An inability to read is likely due to environmental factors – most of the world's population was illiterate a thousand years ago. But an inability to recognize faces is an indication of a serious cognitive deficiency.

Most of the drives and desires of humans can be explained by evolutionary processes. We are intensely social creatures, for example, and are aware of kin and friendship relationships, because we evolved from small bands of hunters and gatherers. We are extremely sensitive to being cheated. On the African savannah, the only way to store the food from a large animal was by sharing it with the group, in anticipation that when one of them faced a similar situation, they would share it in return. Being aware of reciprocity, and being sensitive to cheating, lying and stealing, are basic human traits. The reason is obvious – ancestors who were suckers didn't get enough resources to survive, reproduce and have their children live long enough to reproduce.

Okay, so why the digression into evolutionary psychology. The reason is because a similar argument can be made about financial markets. The ordinary ups and downs of the business cycle have been used to claim that markets are inefficient and capitalism is doomed. But, like human nature, markets are a powerful and durable force in human behavior. The earliest known human settlements left evidence that they traded with their neighbors. Not only was Joseph the first person to describe the business cycle, the entire Bible is filled with references to wealth, poverty and business transactions. One of my favorite of the 613 *mitzvot*[47] is the obligation to use honest weights and measures, to reinforce the idea that one should deal fairly in business matters. Every system that has attempted to improve on free market capitalism has been a failure. Tens of millions of innocent people starved in China and Russia under Communist schemes to revolutionize agriculture. People cheered and wept with joy when the Berlin Wall was torn down.

47 The 613 Jewish commandments contained in the Torah

The simple matter is that markets work. Just like normal humans have an interest in sex and produce culture with sexual content, we also desire gain and fear loss, and the workings of the economy reflect that tension. People respond to financial incentives. It's about as basic a fact of life as possible. And falling prices (and rising prices) have a built in tendency to self-correct. Greed and fear. For the last few years, the housing market has run on fear. But it won't stay that way forever.

A comparison to the stock market. Stocks were hot in the 1960's. Similar to the Internet boom of more recent times, there was a group of sexy companies in the 1960's known as the "Nifty Fifty" that were going to make everyone who owned them rich. They included names such as LTV, Polaroid and Pan Am, all of which eventually filed for bankruptcy, as well as Avon and Xerox, which are still around but have, from an investment standpoint, faded to boring. The Nifty Fifty were also known as "one decision" stocks, the decision in this case being to buy them and then hold them forever.

This strategy resulted in disaster for the unfortunate investors who followed it.

The Dow Jones Industrial Average first closed above 1,000 in 1966, a level it did not reach again until 1982. Over the ensuing sixteen years, the US experienced racial violence and rioting in major cities, massive protests against the Vietnam war, two oil shocks in the 1970's, and the sorry spectacle of the Jimmy Carter presidency, perhaps America's weakest moment.

In the summer of 1982, the Dow traded as low as 770. In nominal terms, meaning not adjusted for inflation, this was a level about 20% below the high point of 1996. In real terms, adjusted for inflation, this meant that stocks had lost about 80% of their value. You may recall that inflation was a serious problem in the 1970's, and the term "stagflation" – high inflation and high unemployment, was coined during this time.

And then, rather suddenly, as if a bell were rung, on August 17, 1982, the Dow Jones Industrial Average rose 5%, which in retrospect can be seen as triggering the longest extended market rise in modern times.[48] It began with a single sharp rally that just never seemed to stop. The Dow eventually went to a high of over 14,000 by early 2000. If you had invested back then in an index fund that simply matched the overall market, you would have earned a return of nearly twenty times your investment.

Nonetheless, that does not mean that everyone who invested in the stock market during this era made a fortune. Many individual stocks performed poorly and every year saw a typical number of corporate bankruptcies that brought stock prices for some companies all the way down to zero. Also, many people did not have the resources to invest in the market, and needed funds for other reasons, such as to pay for college, make a down payment on a house (how quaint!) or chose invest in bonds and annuities to generate a steady monthly income.

So, even if one had a crystal ball in 1982 and knew the market was headed higher, that didn't auto-

---

48 I was in a locker room that day after a round of golf and heard one guy say to another, "Hey, did you hear the stock market was up 38 points today?" Little did I know this was as historically significant a casual remark as I might hear in a lifetime.

matically translate that everyone should own stocks or that every stock was worth owning. I am a big proponent of common sense, and my argument that now is a great time to buy a house and to invest in residential real estate via the stock market does not mean this recommendation is right for every single person or that every house is worth buying.

You still need to do your homework. If you are considering buying a home, you should evaluate whether it's in good condition, located in a community with encouraging economic prospects, near highly rated schools and so on. A former crack house surrounded by abandoned properties in an economically depressed area is probably a bad investment under any circumstances (which is why you can buy a foreclosed home in Detroit for less than the cost of three-year old used car). You also want to ask yourself whether based on life circumstances whether owning a home is a good decision. If you are just starting your career and think you might need to move in a few years to advance professionally, or are not confident about the stability of your job or income level, renting might still be a better choice. You probably don't want to buy a house unless you can reasonably expect to live in it for a minimum of five years, and preferably longer. Or you might like to travel or you just don't want to shoulder the commitment required to maintain a house and property, and find that apartment living is just easier. About two-thirds of Americans own their homes (or did, before the foreclosure crisis – now it seems that banks own an ever-increasing percentage) and about one-third rent. You might be in the one-third, regardless of which direction the housing market is headed in.

Chapter 11: Be Fruitful and Multiply

I am an optimist. It does not seem too much use being anything else.

Winston Churchill

I recently had a discussion about prospects for the economy with my young son-in-law. Despite all the advantages of youth, he was pessimistic about the future while I was optimistic. Isn't it supposed to be the other way around?

Perhaps it is due to environmental factors. I work in high tech, where things only get better with the passage of time. My phone has a GPS as a free app. A few years ago a GPS cost several hundred dollars. A few years before that, people printed out maps from the Internet. A few years before that, people simply got lost.[49]

My son-in-law is a college student, where the faculty is invariably leftist. For college professors, Western

---

49 Maybe the rapid advance of Internet technology is due to men's unwillingness to ask for directions.

civilization and capitalism in particular is always on the brink of collapse. Every day I am surrounded by people who believe the future means progress, while he is surrounded by people for whom the future means decline.

Or perhaps my optimism comes from my Jewish heritage. In Judaism, we believe that the world was created imperfect, and that every person has an obligation to perform *tikkun olam*, or repair of the world. Jews view humanity as God's partner in creation. Two hundred years ago our great nation enslaved millions of African-Americans and oppressed women while celebrating ourselves as a free democracy. Fifty years ago people in industrial centers like Pittsburgh, were grateful for air pollution so thick they could not see the sun because it meant the factories were running at full capacity and jobs were plentiful. On August 28, 1963, in his "I Have a Dream" speech, Dr. Martin Luther King, Jr. stood at the foot of the Washington Monument and told the world that America had given the Negro people a promissory note that came back marked "insufficient funds." Thirty years ago the NYPD raided a popular gay bar, The Stonewall, because gay people had the audacity to exist.

Yes, the world is getting better. People are freer, the air is cleaner, there are more channels on TV, life expectancies have improved and the rate of cosmetic surgery has soared. I even cleaned out two closets recently. Like Churchill, I have never found a better philosophy than optimism. I hope I have persuaded you, dear reader, to share some of mine.

About The Author

Ed Harris is a middle-aged business executive from New York, who now lives with his family in Seattle. He began his career on Wall Street, and since relocating to the West coast over twenty years ago, he has helped create and develop several successful technology companies.

Harris' children, three in number and of assorted genders, skin colors and countries of origin, are united in a common belief that their father was born fully-formed as a grouchy adult. His long-suffering wife bears silent testimony to the saying that "behind every successful man is a surprised woman."

Email the author at: edharris.author@gmail.com